I'm convinced that the Bible is somehow powerfully si complex. Like a diamond viewed from different angles, Scripture continually confronts my heart in fresh ways. This Bible-study series offers insightful perspectives and gives its participants a refreshing opportunity to admire the character of God and be transformed by the truth of his Word. Our souls need to meander through the minutiae and metanarrative of the Bible, and the **Storyline Bible Studies** help us do both.

> KYLE IDLEMAN, senior pastor of Southeast Christian Church and bestselling author of *Not a Fan* and *One at a Time*

If you are longing for a breath of fresh air in your spiritual life, this study is for you. Kat Armstrong brings to life both familiar and less familiar Bible stories in such an engaging way that you can't help but see how the God of the past is also working and moving in your present. Through the captivating truths revealed in this series, you will discover more about God's faithfulness, be equipped to move past fear and disappointment, and be empowered to be who you were created to be. If your faith has felt mundane or routine, these words will be a refreshing balm to your soul and a guide to go deeper in your relationship with God.

> HOSANNA WONG, international speaker and bestselling author of *How (Not) to Save the World: The Truth about Revealing God's Love to the People Right Next to You*

We are watching a new wave of Bible studies that care about the Bible's big story, from Genesis to Revelation; that plunge Bible readers into the depths of human despair and show them the glories of the Kingdom God plans for creation; and that invite readers to participate in that story in all its dimensions—in the mountains and the valleys. Anyone who ponders these Bible studies will come to terms not only with the storyline of the Bible but also with where each of us fits in God's grand narrative. I heartily commend Kat's **Storyline Bible Studies**.

> REV. CANON DR. SCOT MCKNIGHT, professor of New Testament at Northern Seminary

Kat Armstrong is an able trail guide with contagious enthusiasm! In this series, she'll take you hiking through Scripture to experience mountains and valleys, sticks and stones, sinners and saints. If you are relatively new to the Bible or are struggling to see how it all fits together, your trek with Kat will be well worth it. You might even decide that hiking through the Bible is your new hobby.

CARMEN JOY IMES, associate professor of Old Testament at Biola University and author of *Bearing God's Name: Why Sinai Still Matters*

Kat Armstrong takes you into the heart of Scripture so that Scripture can grow in your heart. The **Storyline Bible Studies** have everything: the overarching story of God's redemption, the individual biblical story's historical context, and the text's interpretation that connects with today's realities. Armstrong asks insightful questions that make the Bible come alive and draws authentically on her own faith journey so that readers might deepen their relationship with Jesus. Beautifully written and accessible, the **Storyline Bible Studies** are a wonderful resource for individual or group study.

LYNN H. COHICK, PHD, provost and dean of academic affairs at Northern Seminary

Christians affirm that the Bible is God's Word and provides God's life-giving instruction and encouragement. But what good is such an authoritative and valuable text if God's people don't engage it to find the help the Scriptures provide? Here's where Kat Armstrong's studies shine. In each volume, she presents Bible study as a journey through Scripture that can be transformational. In the process, she enables readers to see the overarching storyline of the Bible and to find their place in that story. In addition, Armstrong reinforces the essential steps that make Bible study life-giving for people seeking to grow in their faith. Whether for individuals, for small groups, or as part of a church curriculum, these studies are ideally suited to draw students into a fresh and invigorating engagement with God's Word.

WILLIAM W. KLEIN, PHD, professor emeritus of New Testament interpretation and author of *Handbook for Personal Bible Study: Enriching Your Experience with God's Word*

Kat has done two things that I love. She's taken something that is familiar and presented it in a fresh way that is understandable by all, balancing the profound with accessibility. And her trustworthy and constant approach to Bible study equips the participant to emerge from this study with the ability to keep studying and growing more.

MARTY SOLOMON, creator and executive producer of *The BEMA Podcast*

You are in for an adventure. In this series, Kat pulls back the curtain to reveal how intentionally God has woven together seemingly disconnected moments in the collective Bible story. Her delivery is both brilliant and approachable. She will invite you to be a curious sleuth as you navigate familiar passages of Scripture, discovering things you'd never seen before. I promise you will never read the living Word the same again.

JENN JETT BARRETT, founder and visionary of The Well Summit

Kat has done it again! The same wisdom, depth, humility, and authenticity that we have come to expect from her previous work is on full display here in her new **Storyline Bible Study** series. Kat is the perfect guide through these important themes and through the story of Scripture: gentle and generous on the one hand, capable and clear on the other. She is a gifted communicator and teacher of God's Word. The format of these studies is helpful too— perfect pacing, just the right amount of new information at each turn, with plenty of space for writing and prayerful reflection as you go and some great resources for further study. I love learning from Kat, and I'm sure you will too. Grab a few friends from your church or neighborhood and dig into these incredible resources together to find your imagination awakened and your faith strengthened.

DAN LOWERY, president of Pillar Seminary

Kat Armstrong possesses something I deeply admire: a sincere and abiding respect for the Bible. Her tenaciousness to know more about her beloved Christ, her commitment to truth telling, and her desire to dig until she mines the deepest gold for her Bible-study readers makes her one of my favorite Bible teachers. I find few that match her scriptural attentiveness and even fewer that embody her humble spirit. This project is stunning, like the rest of her work.

LISA WHITTLE, bestselling author of *Jesus over Everything: Uncomplicating the Daily Struggle to Put Jesus First*, Bible teacher, and podcast host

STONES

**MAKING GOD'S FAITHFULNESS
THE BEDROCK OF YOUR FAITH**

KAT ARMSTRONG

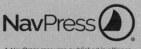

A NavPress resource published in alliance
with Tyndale House Publishers

NavPress®

NavPress is the publishing ministry of The Navigators, an international Christian organization and leader in personal spiritual development. NavPress is committed to helping people grow spiritually and enjoy lives of meaning and hope through personal and group resources that are biblically rooted, culturally relevant, and highly practical.

For more information, visit NavPress.com.

For information about special discounts for bulk purchases, please contact Tyndale House Publishers at csresponse@tyndale.com, or call 1-855-277-9400.

ISBN 978-1-64158-592-7

Printed in the United States of America

29	28	27	26	25	24	23
7	6	5	4	3	2	1

For my dad, Ronald K. Obenhaus.
I think you would have loved this.

Contents

A Message from Kat

RUSSIA INVADED UKRAINE as I started to write this Bible study.

Throughout the invasion, I vacillated between feeling helpless and distraught. Helpless because life felt so fragile and subject to evil's whims. And distraught because the images of Ukrainian children, stumbling across the border to Poland, broke my heart. The sounds of toddlers crying for their daddies and whimpering after a long, harrowing journey was too much for me to bear.

The day before the invasion I was looking up every use of the words *stone* and *rock* in the Bible, and the next day the whole world seemed unprotected, vulnerable, and defenseless. It felt as if the ground beneath my feet were sinking sand, catastrophically damaged, irreparable.

What I needed most during that season of life was to remember that God is faithful. His character is solid as a rock, and I can build my life on the sure foundation of Jesus—who never cracks under pressure. I needed the God described by the psalmists: a stronghold, a refuge, the rock of my salvation, and the rock of my protection.

After some digging in the Scriptures, I was reminded that the Rock of Ages, the one true, living God, is still on his throne (which, according to Revelation, sits in the midst of innumerable precious stones). And Jesus, the Cornerstone of my faith, the surest evidence of God's faithfulness, is still in the business of building his invincible Kingdom—a Kingdom never threatened by evil or evildoers.

If you are struggling to find sure footing in your faith or are longing for security, protection, or refuge, this Bible study will guide you to a hiding place in God. You'll find the safety you long for in your mightiest fortress, Jesus.

Together, we are going to study the bedrock—the foundational principles—of Jacob, Moses, Joshua, Jesus, and the church. What you are going to find in this storyline is that rocks and stones are not random details captured by the Bible's authors. Stone imagery in the Scriptures can build our faith in the same way stones have been used to build altars and memorials of worship.

And the storyline of rocks and stones will lead you to Jesus, the One for whom the stone was rolled away, whose resurrection solidifies our faith.

Love,

Kat

The Storyline of Scripture

YOUR DECISION TO STUDY THE BIBLE for the next few weeks is no accident—God has brought you here, to this moment. And I don't want to take it for granted. Here, at the beginning, I want to invite you into the most important step you can take, the one that brings the whole of the Bible alive in extraordinary ways: a relationship with Jesus.

The Bible is a collection of divinely inspired manuscripts written over fifteen hundred years by at least forty different authors. Together, the manuscripts make up tens of thousands of verses, sixty-six books, and two testaments. Point being: It's a lot of content.

But the Bible is really just one big story: God's story of redemption. From Genesis to Revelation the Bible includes narratives, songs, poems, wisdom literature, letters, and even apocalyptic prophecies. Yet everything we read in God's Word helps us understand God's love and his plan to be in a relationship with us.

If you hear nothing else, hear this: God loves you.

It's easy to get lost in the vast amount of information in the Bible, so we're going to explore the storyline of Scripture in four parts. And as you locate your experience in the story of the Bible, I hope the story of redemption becomes your own.

PART 1: GOD MADE SOMETHING GOOD.

The big story—God's story of redemption—started in a garden. When God launched his project for humanity, he purposed all of us—his image bearers—to flourish and co-create with him. In the beginning there was peace, beauty, order, and abundant life. The soil was good. Life was good. We rarely hear this part of our story, but it doesn't make it less true. God created something good—and that includes you.

PART 2: WE MESSED IT UP.

If you've ever thought, *This isn't how it's supposed to be*, you're right. It's not. We messed up God's good world. Do you ever feel like you've won gold medals in messing things up? Me too. All humanity shares in that brokenness. We are imperfect. The people we love are imperfect. Our systems are jacked, and our world is broken. And that's on us. We made the mess, and we literally can't help ourselves. We need to be rescued from our circumstances, the systems in which we live, and ourselves.

PART 3: JESUS MAKES IT RIGHT.

The good news is that God can clean up all our messes, and he does so through the life, death, and resurrection of Jesus Christ. No one denies that Jesus lived and died. That's just history. It's the empty tomb and the hundreds of eyewitnesses who saw Jesus after his death that make us scratch our heads. Because science can only prove something that is repeatable, we are dependent upon the eyewitness testimonies of Jesus' resurrection for this once-in-history moment. If Jesus rose from the dead—and I believe he did—Jesus is exactly who he said he was, and he accomplished exactly what had been predicted for thousands of years. He restored us. Jesus made *it*, all of it, right. He can forgive your sins and connect you to the holy God through his life, death, and resurrection.

PART 4: ONE DAY, GOD WILL MAKE ALL THINGS NEW.

The best news is that this is not as good as it gets. A day is coming when Christ will return. He's coming back to re-create our world: a place with no tears, no pain, no suffering, no brokenness, no helplessness—just love. God will make all things new. In the meantime, God invites you to step into his storyline, to join him in his work of restoring all things. Rescued restorers live with purpose and on mission: not a life devoid of hardship, but one filled with enduring hope.

RESPONDING TO GOD'S STORYLINE

If the storyline of Scripture feels like a lightbulb turning on in your soul, that, my friend, is the one true, living God, who eternally exists as Father, Son, and Holy Spirit. God is inviting you into a relationship with him to have your sins forgiven and secure a place in his presence forever. When you locate your story within God's story of redemption, you begin a lifelong relationship with God that brings meaning, hope, and restoration to your life.

Take a moment now to begin a relationship with Christ:

God, I believe the story of the Bible, that Jesus is Lord and you raised him from the dead to forgive my sins and make our relationship possible. Your storyline is now my story. I want to learn how to love you and share your love with others. Amen.

If you confess with your lips that Jesus is Lord and believe in your heart that God raised him from the dead, you will be saved.

ROMANS 10:9

How to Use This Bible Study

THE **STORYLINE BIBLE STUDIES** are versatile and can be used for

- individual study (self-paced),
- small groups (five- or ten-lesson curriculum), or
- church ministry (semester-long curriculum).

INDIVIDUAL STUDY

Each lesson in the *Stones* Bible study is divided into four fifteen- to twenty-minute parts (sixty to eighty minutes of individual study time per lesson). You can work through the material one part at a time over a few different days or all in one sitting. Either way, this study will be like anything good in your life: What you put in, you get out. Each of the four parts of each lesson will help you practice Bible-study methods.

SMALL GROUPS

Working through the *Stones* Bible study with a group could be a catalyst for life change. Although the Holy Spirit can teach you truth when you read the Bible on your own, I want to encourage you to gather a small group together to work through this study for these reasons:

- God himself is in communion as one essence and three persons: Father, Son, and Holy Spirit.
- Interconnected, interdependent relationships are hallmarks of the Christian faith life.
- When we collaborate with each other in Bible study, we have access to the viewpoints of our brothers and sisters in Christ, which enrich our understanding of the truth.

For this Bible study, every small-group member will need a copy of the *Stones* study guide. In addition, I've created a free downloadable small-group guide that includes

- discussion questions for each lesson,
- Scripture readings, and
- prayer prompts.

Whether you've been a discussion leader for decades or just volunteered to lead a group for the first time, you'll find the resources you need to create a loving atmosphere for men and women to grow in Christlikeness. You can download the small-group guide using this QR code.

CHURCH MINISTRY

Church and ministry leaders: Your work is sacred. I know that planning and leading through a semester of ministry can be both challenging and rewarding. That's why every **Storyline Bible Study** is written so that you can build modular semesters of ministry. The *Stones* Bible study is designed to complement the *Sticks*

Bible study. Together, *Sticks* and *Stones* can support a whole semester of ministry seamlessly, inviting the people you lead into God's Word and making your life simpler.

To further equip church and ministry leaders, I've created *The Leader's Guide*, a free digital resource. You can download *The Leader's Guide* using this QR code.

The Leader's Guide offers these resources:

- a sample ministry calendar for a ten-plus-lesson semester of ministry,
- small-group discussion questions for each lesson,
- Scripture readings for each lesson,
- prayer prompts for each lesson,
- five teaching topics for messages that could be taught in large-group settings, and
- resources for deeper study.

SPECIAL FEATURES

However you decide to utilize the *Stones* Bible study, whether for individual, self-paced devotional time; as a small-group curriculum; or for semester-long church ministry, you'll notice several stand-out features unique to the **Storyline Bible Studies**:

- gospel presentation at the beginning of each Bible study;
- full Scripture passages included in the study so that you can mark up the text and keep your notes in one place;
- insights from diverse scholars, authors, and Bible teachers;
- an emphasis on close readings of large portions of Scripture;
- following one theme instead of focusing on one verse or passage;
- Christological narrative theology without a lot of church-y words; and
- retrospective or imaginative readings of the Bible to help Christians follow the storyline of Scripture.

You may have studied the Bible by book, topic, or passage before; all those approaches are enriching ways to read the Word of God. The **Storyline Bible Studies** follow a literary thread to deepen your appreciation for God's master plan of redemption and develop your skill in connecting the Old Testament to the New.

THE STONES STORYLINE

STONES ARE SOME OF the most indestructible things in nature. Even when they are destroyed—beaten by weather, ground down, battered, worn by time—they re-form and make something new. They are still stone. They endure.

Perhaps that's why in Scripture, stones are such a profound sign of God's faithfulness. Again and again, when stones show up in the Bible, we see God proving himself to be faithful, loyal in his love, powerful, sacrificial, and purposeful.

And here's the thing: God's faithfulness was not—and is not—dependent on the people he was in relationship with. Many of those we'll read about in this study struggled with feeling unworthy of God's grace. Doubted whether God was as forgiving as he says. Yearned to experience progress in their faith walks. Took steps of obedience when the odds were against them. And needed salvation from their sins. I find parts of my own story in theirs because I, too, am searching for worthiness, forgiveness, progress, rescue, and purpose.

Ultimately, what I learned from the stones of Scripture is that stones are a tangible reminder of God's faithfulness, pointing us again and again to the Rock, to the One for whom the stone was rolled away, to the Living Stone who makes us living stones. God's faithfulness, in the face of our unworthiness, culminates in extravagant grace and the commission to take the beauty of the Kingdom to those around us.

In *Stones*, we're going to explore

- *Genesis 28, 35*: the bedrock of Jacob. Rocks and stones emerge in Jacob's story as the sign of his connection to God and remembrance of God's call on his life.
- *Exodus 34*: the bedrock of Moses. Rocks and stones play a key role in Moses' story as the sign of God's enduring covenant with a stubborn and disobedient people.
- *Joshua 4*: the bedrock of Joshua. Rocks and stones show up in Joshua's story when he has the Israelites bring stones of remembrance together to bear witness to God's faithfulness.
- *Matthew 27–28*: the bedrock of Jesus. The impact of stones in the story of God changes forever when the power of God rolls away the tombstone for the resurrected Christ.
- *1 Peter 2*: the bedrock of the church. Rocks and stones convey our purpose as living stones, commissioned to live out God's purpose in the world.

My favorite part of this storyline is the stone being rolled away from Jesus' tomb when he is raised to life after death. Through it all, again and again, we are reminded: No matter where we are or what we're going through, God's faithfulness endures.

We're going to trace the stones storyline through four different lenses:

- **PART 1: CONTEXT.** Do you ever feel dropped into a Bible story disoriented? Part 1 will introduce you to the stories you're going to study and help you study those stories in their scriptural context. Getting your bearings before you read will enable you to answer the question *What am I about to read?*

- **PART 2: SEEING.** Do you ever read on autopilot? I do too. Sometimes I finish reading without a clue as to what just happened. A better way to read the Bible is to practice thoughtful, close reading of Scripture to absorb the message God is offering to us. That's why part 2 includes close Scripture reading and observation questions to empower you to answer the question *What is the story saying?*

- **PART 3: UNDERSTANDING.** If you've ever scratched your head after reading your Bible, part 3 will give you the tools to understand the author's intended meaning both for the original audience and for you. Plus you'll practice connecting the Old and New Testaments to get a fuller picture of God's unchanging grace. Part 3 will enable you to answer the question *What does it mean?*

- **PART 4: RESPONDING.** The purpose of Bible study is to help you become more Christlike; that's why part 4 will include journaling space for your reflection on and responses to the content and a blank checklist for actionable next steps. You'll be able to process what you're learning so that you can live out the concepts and pursue Christlikeness. Part 4 will enable you to answer the questions *What truths is this passage teaching?* and *How do I apply this to my life?*

One of my prayers for you, as a curious Bible reader, is that our journey through this study will help you cultivate a biblical imagination so that you're able to make connections throughout the whole storyline of the Bible. In each lesson, I'll do my best to include a few verses from different places in the Bible that are connected to our rock and stone motif. At a time when we are so practiced in pulling things out of the Scriptures or apart in our faith, the **Storyline Bible Studies** will help you put things back together.

God's Word is so wonderful, I hardly know how to contain my excitement. Feel free to geek out with me; let your geek flag fly high, my friends. When we can see how interrelated all the parts of Scripture are to each other, we'll find our affection for God stirred as we see his artistic brilliance unfold.

YOUR WORTHINESS COMES FROM GOD'S FAITHFULNESS

BEDROCK OF JACOB:
WHERE JACOB'S FAITH BECOMES HIS OWN

SCRIPTURE: GENESIS 28, 35

PART 1

CONTEXT

Before you begin your study, we will start with the context of the story we are about to read together: the setting, both cultural and historical; the people involved; and where our passage fits in the larger setting of Scripture. All these things help us make sense of what we're reading. Understanding the context of a Bible story is fundamental to reading Scripture well. Getting your bearings before you read will enable you to answer the question *What am I about to read?*

"I'VE MADE A MESS OF MY LIFE, and I'm trying to get my cr** together—but I need to fly under the radar today."

She was a thirtysomething professional wearing a pencil skirt and working the room for new contacts. Between bursts of confidence and introductory smiles, she leaned over and began to whisper her story. She didn't want to take a picture with me at the networking luncheon, she said—not because of the messy divorce she'd just been through, but because she was skittish at the thought of her dad and stepmom, both devout Christians, finding out she'd attended a Christian luncheon.

This young woman was a delight to talk to. She was interesting, ambitious, and open about her faith journey. She had believed in Jesus at one time in her youth, and she really hoped she still had faith, but she was just starting to figure that out on her own. Her dad and stepmom hovered over her at every social event in hopes she would become a churchgoer again. And she felt the pressure to please them. What she really needed was space to explore her faith independently.

At a time when Christians are all abuzz about the next generation leaving the faith in record numbers, this young woman was trying to find her way back without drawing a lot of attention. Like a startled deer, she was wary, concerned that her parents would pounce at any slight movement toward faith in Jesus.

She and I met several times after that luncheon, and each time we were together, she unpacked parts of her story. She was inching back toward Christ and working through what she called "the shame of a failed marriage."

But what she wanted to talk about most was God's faithfulness in spite of our unworthiness. She was shocked to find out that I shared those feelings of unworthiness. I continue, to this day, to feel uneasy about God's undeserved grace. There's a tension between knowing how undeserving I am to be loved by God and accepting that he freely offers his love to me anyway.

This woman and I had little else in common. But the bond we shared is something I'm betting you and I share too: the uneasy appreciation of God's grace.

Fully aware of her faults, her mistakes, and her doubts, the young woman from the luncheon wrestled through them all to embrace God's faithfulness. I'm trying to do the same thing in my own faith journey. It meant a lot to me then that she confided in me. And now, as I reflect on her story, I'm also encouraged that some of our deepest struggles were shared by the brothers and sisters in the faith who came before us.

Much like the young woman at the luncheon, a man in the Bible named Jacob was discovering his faith apart from his very religious parents, Isaac and Rebekah. Jacob came from the most famous faith family in Christian history. God had

> Jacob's life so far had been sheltered. He had been the son who preferred his mother's company and followed her advice. He had shown himself to be an untrustworthy schemer. Now, however, he is thrust out on a new journey, where he will have to learn to survive on his own, without the help of his parents.[1]
>
> Jesudason Baskar Jeyaraj, "Genesis," in *South Asia Bible Commentary*

promised Jacob's grandfather, Abraham, that the blessings intended for everyone in the world would come through Abraham's family. *No pressure.*

And God-fearing parents were not the only thing Jacob shared with my friend from the luncheon. Both of them also had hover mothers who meddled.

To understand Jacob's faith life, you need a little insight into his backstory. But how does one summarize the beginnings of the world as we know it? How could I possibly synthesize the hinge moments in our faith history from Adam and Eve through the line of Abraham to get us all the way to Jacob? The best that we can do for now is acknowledge that Jacob's story in isolation is riveting. But in context, Jacob is a link from God's promise to his grandfather, Abraham, all the way to Jesus.

Jacob is best known for his sneaky ambition, trickster deception, and emotional outbursts.[2] And for some, Jacob's most memorable moment in Scripture is when he schemes to inherit his brother's blessing. The plan Jacob and his mother hatch together works, leaving him with the "blessing" of material and social capital—but bankrupt emotionally and relationally. Jacob runs away from his vengeful brother and ends up distanced from the only life he's ever known. But there, far from the security and familiarity of his familial ties, Jacob has an encounter with God that shapes the rest of his life.

As I researched the bedrock of Jacob's faith, I was surprised by the stone imagery in his story:

- Jacob uses a stone as a pillow at Bethel while he has a dream about God's presence (Genesis 28:11-17).
- Jacob uses the stone to create a memorial at Bethel to commemorate his vision from God (Genesis 28:18-22).
- Jacob rolls a stone away from a well after meeting his future wife, Rachel (Genesis 29:10).
- Jacob builds a stone memorial when entering into an agreement with his father-in-law, Laban (Genesis 31:45-54).
- Jacob creates a pillar of stone at Bethel to renew his covenant with God (Genesis 35:9-14).

Every biblical scholar I referenced talks about the overwhelming role stones play in Jacob's life. Robert Alter, professor in the graduate school and emeritus professor of Hebrew and comparative literature at the University of California at Berkeley, has this to say about Jacob's bedrock of faith:

> Jacob is a man who sleeps on stones, speaks in stones, wrestles with stones, contending with the hard unyielding nature of things.[3]

What you are about to read is one of the episodes in Jacob's life where God's unmerited favor and love are most obvious. As uncomfortable as it makes us all feel, God will reassure Jacob—and, by way of the Scriptures, all of us—that one's worthiness comes from God's faithfulness and nothing else.

1. **PERSONAL CONTEXT: What is going on in your life right now that might impact how you understand this Bible story?**

What a reassurance Jacob's encounter with God offers us today. Despite our limitations and our failings, both as individuals and as his church, God is able to achieve his purposes through us (see 1 Cor 1:26-29).[4]

Jesudason Baskar Jeyaraj, "Genesis," in *South Asia Bible Commentary*

2. **SPIRITUAL CONTEXT: If you've never studied this Bible story before, what piques your curiosity? If you've studied these passages before, what impressions and insights do you recall? What problems or concerns might you have with the story?**

PART 2

SEEING

Seeing the text is vital if we want the heart of the Scripture passage to sink in. We read slowly and intentionally through the text with the context in mind. As we practice close, thoughtful reading of Scripture, we pick up on phrases, implications, and meanings we might otherwise have missed. Part 2 includes close Scripture reading and observation questions to empower you to answer the question *What is the story saying?*

1. Read Genesis 28:10-22 and circle every mention of a stone or rock.

¹⁰ Jacob left Beer-sheba and went toward Haran. ¹¹ He came to a certain place and stayed there for the night, because the sun had set. Taking one of the stones of the place, he put it under his head and lay down in that place. ¹² And he dreamed that there was a ladder set up on the earth, the top of it reaching to heaven; and the angels of God were ascending and descending on it. ¹³ And the LORD stood beside him and said, "I am the LORD, the God of Abraham your father and the God of Isaac; the land on which you lie I will give to you and to your offspring; ¹⁴ and your offspring shall be like the dust of the earth, and you shall spread abroad to the west and to the east and to the north and to the south; and all the families of the earth shall be blessed in you and in your offspring. ¹⁵ Know that I am

with you and will keep you wherever you go, and will bring you back to this land; for I will not leave you until I have done what I have promised you." [16] Then Jacob woke from his sleep and said, "Surely the LORD is in this place—and I did not know it!" [17] And he was afraid, and said, "How awesome is this place! This is none other than the house of God, and this is the gate of heaven."

[18] So Jacob rose early in the morning, and he took the stone that he had put under his head and set it up for a pillar and poured oil on the top of it. [19] He called that place Bethel; but the name of the city was Luz at the first. [20] Then Jacob made a vow, saying, "If God will be with me, and will keep me in this way that I go, and will give me bread to eat and clothing to wear, [21] so that I come again to my father's house in peace, then the LORD shall be my God, [22] and this stone, which I have set up for a pillar, shall be God's house; and of all that you give me I will surely give one tenth to you."

GENESIS 28:10-22

2. According to Genesis 28:11, what did Jacob use a stone for?

The wakeful world of Jacob was a world of fear, terror, loneliness (and, we may imagine, unresolved guilt). Those were parameters of his existence. The dream permits the entry of an alternative into his life. The dream is not a morbid review of a shameful past. It is rather the presentation of an alternative future with God. . . .

The news is that there is traffic between heaven and earth.[5]

Walter Brueggemann, *Genesis*

I'm the kind of gal who travels with her own firm pillow, so Jacob's sleeping arrangement is hard for me to imagine. But it didn't seem to hinder his rest, because he dreamed vividly.

3. **Describe Jacob's dream in the first person, as if you had the dream yourself. How would you share what happened with a friend? Write out what you would text a friend here.**

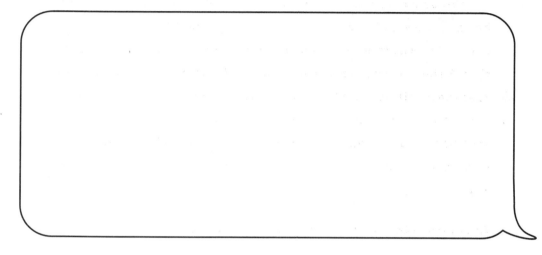

4. **The ladder in Jacob's dream (Gensis 28:12) could represent many different things. List anything you can imagine the symbolism of the ladder might communicate to Jacob.**

My list was rather long, but the answer that stands out is that God presents himself to Jacob in a way that embodies his promise to be with Jacob and watch over him wherever he goes. God makes his faithfulness known at a moment when Jacob likely feels least deserving. As Richard Bauckham notes, "It is not Jacob who turns to God but God who turns to Jacob."[7]

Isn't it just like God? He assures Jacob he will be with him in the future by making his presence real in Jacob's present. This holds true in our faith life too—we can be hopeful and confident of God's character because of what he has done in our past. I'm certain God chose this moment and this method of revelation so that Jacob would know what it is to have his dreams come true.

5. Write out what God says to Jacob.

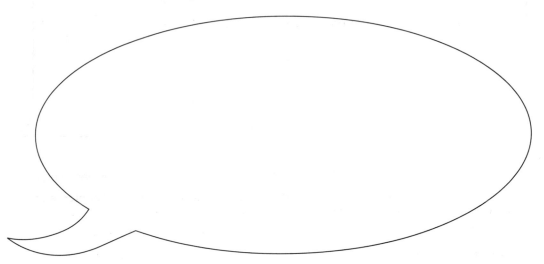

He names the place Bethel, which means "the house of God." But even this recognition of God's presence there at Bethel does not reach the deepest meaning of Jacob's dream. What he has discovered is not so much that God is in that particular place as that God is where Jacob is.[6]

Richard Bauckham, *Who Is God?*

6. **How does Jacob respond to his dream? Check all that apply.**

☐ He wakes up confident that God's presence is near.

☐ He wakes up confused.

☐ He wakes up afraid.

☐ He wakes up in awe that heaven and earth meet at the place where he has been sleeping.

☐ He sets up the stone he used as a pillow as a memorial of God's covenant.

☐ He ignores the dream and moves on with his life.

☐ He names the place Luz.

☐ He names the place Bethel.

☐ He makes a vow that his family's God will be his own.

7. **How do you think you would have responded to Jacob's dream?**

A lot happens between Genesis 28, where Jacob uses a stone as a pillow and dreams of God's presence, and the next passage we're going to read. I wish I could tell you that Jacob's life after Bethel was a happy ending. But you and I know better. Life is a series of ups and downs, and Jacob certainly rode the roller coaster of trusting God.

One of the most disturbing episodes in Jacob's story is in Genesis 34, when a man named Shechem rapes Jacob's daughter Dinah. In my book *The In-Between Place*, I spend a considerable amount of ink unpacking this tragedy and how cowardly Jacob behaves.[8] When Jacob hears about Dinah's rape, he is silent. From what we see in the text, Jacob seems unconcerned that Dinah has lived through such trauma.

There's more to this story that we can't cover in our study time, but I'm bringing your attention to this dark episode because it happens right before the next section of Scripture we are going to study together. In this passage, Jacob is coming off the heels of his daughter's rape and his sons' revenge—the mass murder of all the people living in the town where Dinah was assaulted. Jacob is once again suffering from shame because he knows he is not worthy of God's covenant with him made back at Bethel.

But notice with me how Jacob finds solace.

8. Read Genesis 35:1-15 and circle each mention of a stone or rock.

35 God said to Jacob, "Arise, go up to Bethel, and settle there. Make an altar there to the God who appeared to you when you fled from your brother Esau." ² So Jacob said to his household and to all who were with him, "Put away the foreign gods that are among you, and purify yourselves, and change your clothes; ³ then come, let us go up to Bethel, that I may make an altar there to the God who answered me in the day of my distress and has been with me wherever I have gone." ⁴ So they gave to Jacob all the foreign gods that they had, and the rings that were in their ears; and Jacob hid them under the oak that was near Shechem.

⁵ As they journeyed, a terror from God fell upon the cities all around them, so that no one pursued them. ⁶ Jacob came to Luz (that is, Bethel), which is in the land of Canaan, he and all the people who were with him, ⁷ and there he built an altar and called the place El-bethel, because it was there that God had revealed himself to him when he fled from his brother. ⁸ And Deborah, Rebekah's nurse, died, and she was buried under an oak below Bethel. So it was called Allon-bacuth.

⁹ God appeared to Jacob again when he came from Paddan-aram, and he blessed him. ¹⁰ God said to him, "Your name is Jacob; no longer shall you be called Jacob, but Israel shall be your name." So he was called

Israel. ¹¹ God said to him, "I am God Almighty: be fruitful and multiply; a nation and a company of nations shall come from you, and kings shall spring from you. ¹² The land that I gave to Abraham and Isaac I will give to you, and I will give the land to your offspring after you." ¹³ Then God went up from him at the place where he had spoken with him. ¹⁴ Jacob set up a pillar in the place where he had spoken with him, a pillar of stone; and he poured out a drink offering on it, and poured oil on it. ¹⁵ So Jacob called the place where God had spoken with him Bethel.

GENESIS 35:1-15

9. **What does God do in this part of the story? Write out the first five words of Genesis 35:9.**

10. **Do you think Jacob was expecting God to do that? Why or why not?**

Never would I ever expect God to respond to Jacob's failures with such kindness. I've been following Jesus for over twenty years, and I'm still caught by surprise when God is gracious—even though he has proved that that is who he is.

11. List at least three ways a name change for Jacob would have impacted his life.

I wonder how difficult it would have been for the people in Jacob's life to start referring to him as Israel. How many times did they stumble over his name or edit their words to reflect the change? Moving to a new name after a lifetime of another would have been no small adjustment. I am confident that each and every time he heard or used his name, he would think of God's renaming him for his new future.

12. Reread Genesis 35:14. What does Jacob do in response to God's promises?

God didn't instruct Jacob to construct an altar built from the stone[9]—Jacob seems to have done that out of instinct. Jacob needed a tangible reminder of his experience with God. We all need tangible reminders of God's faithfulness, pointing us to Christ and reminding us whose we are, as we walk through this life of faith.

13. What do you think was going through Jacob's mind as he set up the stone pillar?

Jacob's encounter with God in Genesis 28 comes by way of a dream, and then, just chapters later, Jacob and his daughter Dinah live through a nightmare. I believe God made sure the editors of the book of Genesis would show readers like you and me that God is faithful in every circumstance—in our dreams, through our nightmares, and in our daily reality, too. No part of our lived experience happens apart from God's presence.

If you are searching for some tangible evidence that God loves you, that he is watching over you, let Jacob's story and stone memorials serve as evidence. If this is what God is willing to do for someone like Jacob, what is he doing for you?

UNDERSTANDING

Now that we've finished a close reading of the Scriptures, we're going to spend some time on interpretation: doing our best to understand what God was saying to the original audience and what he's teaching us through the process. But to do so, we need to learn his ways and consider how God's Word would have been understood by the original audience before apply-ing the same truths to our own lives. "Scripture interpretation" may sound a little stuffy, but understanding what God means to communicate to us in the Bible is crucial to enjoying a close relationship with Jesus. Part 3 will enable you to answer the question *What does it mean?*

1. **Reread Genesis 28:10-22 and put a box around any mention of the words *you* or *your*.**

¹⁰ Jacob left Beer-sheba and went toward Haran. ¹¹ He came to a certain place and stayed there for the night, because the sun had set. Taking one of the stones of the place, he put it under his head and lay down in that place. ¹² And he dreamed that there was a ladder set up on the earth, the top of it reaching to heaven; and the angels of God were ascending and descending on it. ¹³ And the LORD stood beside him and said, "I am the LORD, the God of Abraham your father and the God of Isaac; the land on which you lie I will give to you and to your offspring; ¹⁴ and your offspring

shall be like the dust of the earth, and you shall spread abroad to the west and to the east and to the north and to the south; and all the families of the earth shall be blessed in you and in your offspring. [15] Know that I am with you and will keep you wherever you go, and will bring you back to this land; for I will not leave you until I have done what I have promised you." [16] Then Jacob woke from his sleep and said, "Surely the LORD is in this place—and I did not know it!" [17] And he was afraid, and said, "How awesome is this place! This is none other than the house of God, and this is the gate of heaven."

[18] So Jacob rose early in the morning, and he took the stone that he had put under his head and set it up for a pillar and poured oil on the top of it. [19] He called that place Bethel; but the name of the city was Luz at the first. [20] Then Jacob made a vow, saying, "If God will be with me, and will keep me in this way that I go, and will give me bread to eat and clothing to wear, [21] so that I come again to my father's house in peace, then the LORD shall be my God, [22] and this stone, which I have set up for a pillar, shall be God's house; and of all that you give me I will surely give one tenth to you."

GENESIS 28:10-22

2. **God's message to Jacob seems to focus on God's connection to Jacob's family, but it also emphasizes God's relationship with Jacob. Based on what you know about Jacob, why do you think this would have meant so much to him?**

3. God's people, throughout the Scriptures, lived through some very high highs and very low lows. How do you think reading about Jacob's story would have strengthened their faith?

4. Describe a time in your faith journey when you sensed God's presence. How did you know he was near? What caught your attention? How did you respond to that encounter?

5. Reread Genesis 35:1-15 and put a box around any mention of the words *you* or *your*.

35 God said to Jacob, "Arise, go up to Bethel, and settle there. Make an altar there to the God who appeared to you when you fled from your brother Esau." ² So Jacob said to his household and to all who were with him, "Put away the foreign gods that are among you, and purify yourselves, and change your clothes; ³ then come, let us go up to Bethel, that I may make an altar there to the God who answered me in the day of my distress and has been with me wherever I have gone." ⁴ So they gave to Jacob all the foreign gods that they had, and the rings that were in their ears; and Jacob hid them under the oak that was near Shechem.

⁵ As they journeyed, a terror from God fell upon the cities all around them, so that no one pursued them. ⁶ Jacob came to Luz (that is, Bethel), which is in the land of Canaan, he and all the people who were with him, ⁷ and there he built an altar and called the place El-bethel, because it was there that God had revealed himself to him when he fled from his brother. ⁸ And Deborah, Rebekah's nurse, died, and she was buried under an oak below Bethel. So it was called Allon-bacuth.

⁹ God appeared to Jacob again when he came from Paddan-aram, and he blessed him. ¹⁰ God said to him, "Your name is Jacob; no longer shall you be called Jacob, but Israel shall be your name." So he was called Israel. ¹¹ God said to him, "I am God Almighty: be fruitful and multiply; a nation and a company of nations shall come from you, and kings shall spring from you. ¹² The land that I gave to Abraham and Isaac I will give to you, and I will give the land to your offspring after you." ¹³ Then God went up from him at the place where he had spoken with him. ¹⁴ Jacob set up a pillar in the place where he had spoken with him, a pillar of stone; and he poured out a drink offering on it, and poured oil on it. ¹⁵ So Jacob called the place where God had spoken with him Bethel.

GENESIS 35:1-15

> The arrival at Bethel marked the end of Jacob's journey and the final demonstration of God's faithfulness. He had been with Jacob throughout his journey, and now Jacob had returned to Bethel in safety.¹⁰
>
> John H. Sailhamer, *The Pentateuch as Narrative*

My favorite word in my favorite sentence in my favorite paragraph of Genesis 35 is *again*. Again God appears to Jacob. Again God blesses Jacob. Again God renews his covenant with Jacob and his family. Again God shows who he is—he is love.

If you have any doubts about your relationship with Christ, notice that God's pattern is to move toward us in our darkest moments. He will do the same for you. And then he will do it *again*.

MAKING CONNECTIONS

An important part of understanding the meaning of a Bible passage is getting a sense of its place in the broader storyline of Scripture. When we make connections between different parts of the Bible, we get a glimpse of the unity and cohesion of the Scriptures.

When my son, Caleb, was a toddler, he would ask me the same question every time I'd drop him off at preschool or church: "Will you be with me?" His endearing, squeaky tone could make any Scrooge smile. And I think that question is one we all ask God even as we grow into adults. *Will God be with me? Will he be with me through my darkest valleys? Will he turn away from me when I make my poorest decisions? Will God choose to stay with me when it seems like everyone else leaves?*

In the same way Caleb needed the reassurance of my presence, I believe you and I are searching for reassurance in our faith walk with God. Jacob needed consolation too. That's why God intentionally gave confidence-producing messages to Jacob like "I am with you and will keep you wherever you go" (Genesis 28:15).

Fast-forward hundreds of years. God's people are awaiting a Messiah who will fulfill the promises God made to Abraham and Isaac. Jesus enters the storyline of Scripture as the One who can fulfill the promises. Jesus' life, death, and resurrection prompt spiritual renewal led by Jesus' disciples. Before Jesus ascends into heaven, he leaves his disciples with these comforting words:

> [16] Now the eleven disciples went to Galilee, to the mountain to which Jesus had directed them. [17] When they saw him, they worshiped him; but some doubted. [18] And Jesus came and said to them, "All authority in heaven and on earth has been given to me. [19] Go therefore and make disciples of all nations, baptizing them in the name of the Father and of the Son and

of the Holy Spirit, [20] and teaching them to obey everything that I have commanded you. And remember, I am with you always, to the end of the age."

MATTHEW 28:16-20

One of my favorite New Testament scholars, Richard Bauckham, explains the connection between Jacob's experience and that of Jesus' disciples:

> The promise of an accompanying presence of God that would never fail, first given to Jacob, is now renewed and extended, by implication, to the nations that become Jacob's offspring through faith in the Messiah. This happens through a form of the divine presence that Jacob could never have anticipated: the presence of God in the midst of human life *as* the human Jesus, Jacob's own descendant, who thus brings blessing to the nations. Jesus himself is God-with-us.[11]

6. Why does God's staying presence mean so much to Jacob and the disciples?

7. What does it mean to you that God is the with-us God?

One of the ways the enemy gets under my skin is by isolating me. He fakes me out into believing I am alone in my struggles: *No one would understand. No one would want to be my companion as I walk the lonely road.* Nothing could be further from the truth. But try telling me this when I am doubting God or feeling afraid. Both Jacob and the disciples felt fear, and all of them must have been doubting. How does God challenge his people to keep going and encourage us to have faith? He promises to go with us, to ever be the One by our side, through thick and thin.

* * *

In every lesson we'll expand our storyline chart to trace the stone imagery we're studying together.

THE STONES STORYLINE OF SCRIPTURE

Bedrock Scripture(s)	Stone Imagery	God's Faithfulness
bedrock of Jacob (Genesis 28, 35)	stone pillow and pillars of stone (altars)	God is faithful to be with us always.
bedrock of Moses (Exodus 34)	two stone tablets	God is faithful to love us no matter what.
bedrock of Joshua (Joshua 4)	stones of remembrance	God is faithful to help us make progress.
bedrock of Jesus (Matthew 27–28)	the stone that was rolled away from Jesus' empty tomb	God is faithful to conquer sin and death.
bedrock of the church (1 Peter 2)	the Living Stone and living stones	God is faithful to make us living stones.

God's Encouragement	God's Transforming Power	Jesus' Fulfillment of the Stones
"I am with you" (Genesis 28:15).	God opens up a path from heaven to earth to be with Jacob.	Jesus tells his disciples, "I am with you always, to the end of the age" (Matthew 28:20).
"The LORD . . . abounding in steadfast love and faithfulness, keeping steadfast love for the thousandth generation" (Exodus 34:6–7).	God keeps his covenant with us even when we are unfaithful.	Paul says that because of Jesus, "you are a letter of Christ . . . written . . . not on tablets of stone but on tablets of human hearts" (2 Corinthians 3:3).
"Let your children know . . . so that all the peoples of the earth may know that the hand of the LORD is mighty, and so that you may fear the LORD your God forever" (Joshua 4:22, 24).	God parts the Jordan River and leads the Israelites across.	Jesus is the new Joshua who fulfills the law of Moses.
"Do not be afraid" (Matthew 28:10).	God's angel rolls away the stone.	Jesus is "the resurrection and the life" (John 11:25).
"Now you are God's people" (1 Peter 2:10).	God transforms us into his witnesses.	Jesus is the Living Stone, the ultimate witness of God's power and grace.

1. Where do you need to be reminded of God's past faithfulness right now? How can you remind yourself of his faithfulness in what you're facing this week?

2. What did you learn about God's character in this lesson?

3. How should these truths shape your faith community and change you?

RESPONDING

The purpose of Bible study is to help you become more Christlike; that's why part 4 will include journaling space for your reflection on and responses to the content and a blank checklist for actionable next steps. You'll be able to process what you're learning so that you can live out the concepts and pursue Christlikeness. Part 4 will enable you to answer the questions *What truths is this passage teaching?* and *How do I apply this to my life?*

IF YOU'VE HEARD ABOUT the gift-giving principle *give gifts you'd love to receive*, you'll understand my mom's Christmas present this past year. I gave her Philip Yancey's memoir, *Where the Light Fell*, for Christmas—and after she finished reading the book, she lent it to me.

On a weekend when I should have been writing this Bible study, I found myself glued to Yancey's memoir. It gave me a window into his early childhood and his coming to faith in Christ. I hadn't known that the grace he speaks and teaches about, the grace he explores in all his works, was born out of pain, abuse, and trauma. His words of beauty came from an ash heap. Which I find outrageously encouraging.

At an early age Philip recognized that his outward behavior and inward beliefs didn't align. He describes feeling empty, sensing that he was not worthy of God's goodness. And this wasn't wrong—in the sense that he wasn't worthy *on his own*.

Through God's amazing grace, Philip found Christ, Someone he'd heard about all his life but barely knew. And in his spiritual awakening, Philip released the burden of feeling not good enough for God or his terribly abusive mother. Can you imagine the toll it would have taken, enduring a lifetime of believing he was unworthy of God's love and his mother's? Thank God he found Jesus and learned what's so amazing about grace. Decades later, Yancey is still testifying to God's undeserved and unconditional love.

As I read Yancey's memoir and studied Jacob's life, I noticed just how much the two men's stories have in common. Both left their homes and entered a world of unknown. And there, apart from family and riddled with shame, they encountered God's presence and holiness. Both men started their relationships with God through dreamlike revelations and woke up to find their realities reframed by God's promises to journey with them through life's ups and downs.

Your story may not be as severe as Yancey's or Jacob's, but we all grapple with our finitude. How can we please a holy God, let alone serve him faithfully? I have good news for you: Your worthiness comes from God's faithfulness—and nothing else.

1. YOUR WORTHINESS DOES NOT COME FROM YOUR BEHAVIOR.

Jacob's story has an important message for any of us struggling with being

- deceptive,
- manipulative,
- self-absorbed,
- cowardly,
- overly ambitious,
- inconsistent in our relationships,
- overly emotional, or
- at odds with our families.

Jacob acted in ways that were harmful to himself and to others. Jacob distanced himself from his family and from God. And still God approached Jacob, spent time with him, promised Jacob he could count on his presence, encouraged Jacob with his love and kindness, and remained faithful to his promises.

God will do the same for you. He is always approaching you. When it feels like he's far away, he's actually right by your side. When you feel lonely, excluded, ignored, or uninvited, God reaches out to welcome you into his family and befriend you with incomparable loyalty. When the world is closing in on you and you feel helpless, God is making a way for you to continue on because he is guiding you with his nearness. When you feel defeated, unlovable, or ashamed, God offers you his unconditional love and unearned grace. Your worthiness does not come from your behavior—it comes from God's faithfulness.

2. YOUR WORTHINESS DOES NOT COME FROM YOUR FAMILY.

Although God's promises to Jacob were an extension and fulfillment of God's promises to Abraham, none of the people in Jacob's family were worthy of God's faithfulness *in and of themselves*. Jacob's worthiness was not a result of his father's or grandfather's goodness. Correspondingly, Jacob's children and their children are not a reflection of his value.

None of our own families are perfect either. Whether your family was centered on Jesus or not, your worthiness is not connected to where you came from. Maybe your heart aches to have a family of your own and you feel like being single, divorced, or widowed disqualifies you from being a full member of God's Kingdom. Nothing could be further from the truth. Your worthiness does not come from any other person. If you have prodigal children: Your worthiness does not come from their adherence to the Christian faith. If you struggle with infertility: Your worthiness is not birthed through parenthood.

Your worthiness does not come from *your* family—it comes from being part of God's family. Worthiness is a privilege that comes to us through the righteousness of Christ.

3. YOUR WORTHINESS DOES NOT COME FROM YOUR FAITHFULNESS.

Whether you've been a Christian for a few days or several decades, you probably realize that we don't just need grace in coming to faith in Christ—we need grace every single day of our lives. Until Christ returns and remakes the world, you and I are going to feel as though following Christ faithfully is as heavy a burden as a stone boulder. The good news is that none of us have to move that boulder on our own. And our worthiness isn't dependent on our ability to walk the straight and narrow. That truth is not a license to sin, of course. But my point is this: If God was faithful to Jacob, he will be faithful to you. And what made Jacob worthy of God's dependability? Nothing he did himself. Jacob's worthiness came from God's faithfulness. And so does yours.

Use this journaling space to process what you are learning.

Ask yourself how these truths impact your relationship with God and with others.

What is the Holy Spirit bringing to your mind as actionable next steps in your faith journey?

-
-
-

YOUR FORGIVENESS COMES FROM GOD'S STEADFAST LOVE

BEDROCK OF MOSES:
WHERE MOSES ASKS GOD'S FORGIVENESS

SCRIPTURE: EXODUS 34

PART 1

CONTEXT

Before you begin your study, we will start with the context of the story we are
about to read together: the setting, both cultural and historical; the people
involved; and where our passage fits in the larger setting of Scripture. All
these things help us make sense of what we're reading. Understanding the
context of a Bible story is fundamental to reading Scripture well. Getting
your bearings before you read will enable you to answer the question *What
am I about to read?*

MY SISTER-IN-LAW LEE is also my best friend. She tried persuading
me to visit Branson, Missouri, for ages, and I was less than eager to travel some-
where unfamiliar. But Lee was right. The year our family went to Branson for
spring break, we had a blast. If you've never been, it's kind of like Christian
Vegas. Everywhere you turn there are family-friendly amusement parks, shows,
and entertainment.

Many of the conversations we enjoyed with the locals revealed who was re-
sponsible for most of the fun in Branson and the surrounding areas: Johnny
Morris. You may recognize his name as the owner of Bass Pro Shops. Your sister
Kat Armstrong does not shop at Bass Pro. I have no idea what they sell or why.
And I'd never heard of Johnny Morris. But based on what I saw in Branson, Bass
Pro Shops and Johnny Morris are doing real well.

I spent the majority of our road trip from Dallas to Branson looking up every time *stone* or *rock* is used in the Bible. Little did I know that our family was about to visit one of the most famous parts of Branson, Johnny Morris's Top of the Rock Ozarks Heritage Preserve. Less than twenty-four hours after making notes on every use of the word *rock* in the Bible, I was marveling at the pink sunset melting over the lake as we ate dinner at the Top of the Rock. I could have done without the firing of the Civil War cannon, but the rest of the experience is etched into my mind as the second most beautiful sunset I've ever seen.

Thankfully, my family didn't have to hike up Top of the Rock dressed in our Sunday best. Instead, we traveled by car and electric cart. As I cruised up to the famous high point, my mind wandered back to my Bible-study research, all that imagery of rocks and stones in Scripture. I pictured Moses climbing up Mount Sinai with two stone tablets and imagined how difficult his climb must have been compared to our joyride up to the Top of the Rock.

God launched our world so that everyone in it would flourish. That's part of the reason he chose Adam and Eve and then later Abraham and his family—to bring blessings to all people. They were intended to be God's conduits for universal blessing.

> Moses had broken the first two tablets in a symbolic acting indicating that the Israelites had broken their covenant with Yahweh by their idolatry (32:19). Now, the Lord again takes the initiative, this time to remake the covenant. His doing this is symbolised by remaking the stone tablets.[1]
>
> P. G. George and Paul Swarup, "Exodus," in *South Asia Bible Commentary*

Sadly, none of the people chosen by God to represent him lived up to their calling perfectly. Which eventually leads us to the book of Exodus, the second book in the Old Testament Scriptures. The rescue that didn't find its fulfillment in the patriarchs continued in a man named Moses. He, too, was chosen by God to help rescue God's people and bring blessings to the whole world.

We are first introduced to Moses in the book of Exodus, when God's people are enslaved by the Egyptians. The Israelites cry out to God for help, and he sends Moses to lead them out of Egypt, across the Red Sea, and into the Promised Land of freedom. After the miraculous intervention of God, Moses and the Israelites successfully leave Egypt and end up at Mount Sinai on their way to the Promised Land. There, at Mount Sinai, God initiates a legal agreement between himself and his people, pledging to remain faithful. He asks them to follow several laws, all of which are designed to help everyone flourish.

How does God choose to ratify this agreement? He descends on Mount Sinai in a terrifying storm and then invites Moses up the mountain, where he gives Moses a copy of the Ten Commandments. According to Scripture, those laws were etched onto two stone tablets.

While Moses is still on the mountain receiving the stone tablets, God's recently rescued people throw an epic, idolatrous party to worship their newly minted idol, a calf made of gold. Their bright idea is a dark, ominous act of disobedience. The irony is that while God is setting in stone the commandments to have no other gods before him and not to worship idols, the Israelites are doing just that.

The two stone tablets upon which God writes the Ten Commandments are only one significant part of the stones storyline in Moses' life.

- *Exodus 17*: Soon after the Exodus, Moses fears that the grumbling, thirsty Israelites will stone him to death. God provides a solution by instructing Moses to strike a rock for water. Stoning people to death was a barbaric but common way to punish people in that time. What's interesting about this part of Moses' story is that stones are both the weapon of his potential death (Exodus 17:4) and the means by which he is saved from the crowd's fury (Exodus 17:5-6). Later, in the New Testament, the apostle Paul will explain that Jesus is the rock that Moses strikes for the water (1 Corinthians 10:4).

- *Exodus 31 and 34*: God gives the Ten Commandments to Moses on stone tablets.

- *Exodus 28*: When God gives Moses plans for the Tabernacle and specifications for worshiping in it, he includes instructions to put onyx stones on the priests' garments to memorialize the twelve tribes of Israel (Exodus

28:9-12). Every time a priest suits up to serve in the Tabernacle, he will be clothing himself with physical reminders of God's faithfulness to the Israelites. And one of the elements of the priestly garments is a breastplate inlaid with twelve precious stones, which also represented Israel's twelve tribes (Exodus 28:17-21).

- *Exodus 32*: When he realizes the Israelites are worshiping a golden calf, Moses breaks the first set of two stone tablets as a way to symbolize their rebellion (Exodus 32:19).

- *Numbers 20*: Ironically, the reason Moses does not get to enter the Promised Land is that he strikes a rock in the desert twice to get water from it instead of merely speaking to the rock and trusting God to provide (Numbers 20:8-12).

At every turn of Moses' life, we find stone imagery linking the story together as one cohesive whole. Unless you are looking for the repetition, you might miss the significance of the motif, but once you see the pattern, it's impossible to ignore.

What you are about to read is a scene from Moses' life—a story of forgiveness. Maybe like me, you sense an ever-increasing need to be forgiven. At times, I am ashamed of my actions and mortified by my unspoken judgments. Other times, the corrosive nature of resentment has me eager to become more forgiving. But this is our reality: Left up to us, this world would be in a much bigger mess because we are neither prone to forgive nor practiced at receiving forgiveness.

The good news is that God is wholly unlike us in this regard. One of God's unchanging characteristics is being compassionate and loving. He forgives generously.

1. **PERSONAL CONTEXT: What is going on in your life right now that might impact how you understand this Bible story?**

2. **SPIRITUAL CONTEXT: If you've never studied this Bible story before, what piques your curiosity? If you've studied this passage before, what impressions and insights do you recall? What problems or concerns might you have with the passage?**

SEEING

Seeing the text is vital if we want the heart of the Scripture passage to sink in. We read slowly and intentionally through the text with the context in mind. As we practice close, thoughtful reading of Scripture, we pick up on phrases, implications, and meanings we might otherwise have missed. Part 2 includes close Scripture reading and observation questions to empower you to answer the question *What is the story saying?*

1. **Read Exodus 34:1-10, circling every mention of stones or rocks.**

34 The LORD said to Moses, "Cut two tablets of stone like the former ones, and I will write on the tablets the words that were on the former tablets, which you broke. ² Be ready in the morning, and come up in the morning to Mount Sinai and present yourself there to me, on the top of the mountain. ³ No one shall come up with you, and do not let anyone be seen throughout all the mountain; and do not let flocks or herds graze in front of that mountain." ⁴ So Moses cut two tablets of stone like the former ones; and he rose early in the morning and went up on Mount Sinai, as the LORD had commanded him, and took in his hand the two tablets of stone. ⁵ The LORD descended in the cloud and stood with him there, and proclaimed the name, "The LORD." [6] The LORD passed before him, and proclaimed,

> "The LORD, the LORD,
> a God merciful and gracious,
> slow to anger,
> and abounding in steadfast love and faithfulness,
> [7] keeping steadfast love for the thousandth generation,
> forgiving iniquity and transgression and sin,
> yet by no means clearing the guilty,
> but visiting the iniquity of the parents
> upon the children
> and the children's children,
> to the third and the fourth generation."

[8] And Moses quickly bowed his head toward the earth, and worshiped. [9] He said, "If now I have found favor in your sight, O Lord, I pray, let the Lord go with us. Although this is a stiff-necked people, pardon our iniquity and our sin, and take us for your inheritance."

[10] He said: I hereby make a covenant. Before all your people I will perform marvels, such as have not been performed in all the earth or in any nation; and all the people among whom you live shall see the work of the LORD; for it is an awesome thing that I will do with you.

EXODUS 34:1-10

As God passes by Moses and Moses sees the back side of God, God proclaims one of the most significant theological descriptions of the character of God in the entire Old Testament: "The LORD, the LORD, a God merciful and gracious, slow to anger . . . forgiving iniquity and transgression and sin, yet by no means clearing the guilty" (34:6-7).[2]

Dennis T. Olson, "Exodus," in *Theological Bible Commentary*

2. **How do you think Moses "cut two tablets of stone" (Exodus 34:4)?**

I'm trying to wrap my mind around how Moses was able to cut stone tablets without modern power tools. Did this process involve chipping away at a stone structure on a mountain, using only the primitive instruments of wilderness wanderers? Did Moses spend hours or a whole day shaping the tablets? And how big were they? We can't know for sure, but I think the imagery should communicate to us that these few words on the page involved labor.

3. **This is the second time Moses has gone up the mountain to receive the Ten Commandments. What do you think Moses would have been thinking during this second law-giving ceremony?**

If it were me, I'd be doing some internal blame shifting. When God references the "former tablets" and reminds Moses that he is the one who broke them, I would have been talking to myself: *Those people you entrusted me to lead—they broke the laws!*

4. List every detail we are given in Exodus 34:5 about the way God appears to Moses here.

I have to wonder if the details about God's movement onto the mountain reflect more than what happened materially. I wonder if God's coming down is also a reflection of how he lowers himself to be with us in our spiritual relationship with Christ. God is always approaching us, reaching out to us, getting close to us.

5. List everything you learn about God's character from Exodus 34:6-7.

-
-
-
-
-
-
-

In our next lesson we're going to explore the tension between God's mercy and his justice, but for now, go back to the list you just created and circle the characteristics of God that you appreciate the most.

6. How does Moses respond to this conversation with God (Exodus 34:8)? Why do you think he reacts this way?

Moses' reaction could be instructive to each of us. Do you think you would have responded in the same way? I think I, too, would have had the instinct to get as low as possible, a posture to express my gratitude and shock.

7. Write out Moses' three requests of God in Exodus 34:9:

1.

2.

3.

Moses wanted to know the same thing Jacob wanted to know: Would God be with him? I have the same question too. Will God be present in all my highs and lows and everything in between? Will my life be too messy or mundane for God to care about?

Moses, like Jacob, needed assurance. And maybe that is an encouragement to you in this moment. If you need assurance, you are not alone. Sometimes we need to know that we know that God will be our companion, no matter what.

8. **According to Exodus 34:10, how does God intend to perform marvelous things? Check the correct answer:**

   ☐ for us

   ☐ in spite of us

   ☐ on behalf of us

   ☐ with us

The one true, living God wants to involve us in his sacred work of redemption. He wants us to participate with him. It isn't that he needs us, as if he can't accomplish his purposes on his own. No, he *wants* to include us in his work of redemption. He wants you to join his Kingdom work in the same way he wanted the people in this Exodus story to join him. No matter how we might mess things up along the way, God wants to do good works *with us.*

UNDERSTANDING

Now that we've finished a close reading of the Scriptures, we're going to spend some time on interpretation: doing our best to understand what God was saying to the original audience and what he's teaching us through the process. But to do so, we need to learn his ways and consider how God's Word would have been understood by the original audience before applying the same truths to our own lives. "Scripture interpretation" may sound a little stuffy, but understanding what God means to communicate to us in the Bible is crucial to enjoying a close relationship with Jesus. Part 3 will enable you to answer the question *What does it mean?*

MOSES' CONVERSATION WITH GOD in Exodus 34:1-10 comes after the blatant rebellion of God's people. Just moments before God declares himself the merciful God who is slow to anger, the Israelites put God's patience to the test. Right before God announces to Moses that he is abounding in steadfast love and faithfulness, God's people prove that they abound in neither love nor faithfulness. The entire covenant renewal is necessary because the Israelites have broken the covenant in the first place.

Don't miss this important truth: *Even when we break our part of the agreement, God keeps his.* God will allow you and me to experience the consequences of our sins, but even when we turn our backs on him, he doesn't abandon his promise to bless all people.

1. **What about this story would have encouraged the Israelites? How would a covenant-renewal story impact their faith in God?**

In lesson one we looked closely at a scene from Jacob's life in Genesis 35 when God renews a covenant near Bethel. First God makes a covenant, then the actions of God's people seem to threaten it. But by his grace, he upholds the original agreement and even renews it. God's behavior is creating a unifying pattern in these narratives: He is the God of second chances.

If you know what it is to regret your decisions and wish you could have a life mulligan, a do-over, guess what? God is generously forgiving. He specializes in second chances. Jacob didn't exhaust God's mercy, and neither did Moses. None of the people being led by either of those men exhausted God's mercy either. There is hope for us yet.

2. **Who is the most merciful person in your life? What about the most justice oriented? Are they the same person? Why or why not?**

In my own life, the person who is most merciful and the one who is most justice oriented are not only different people; they are polar opposites. It is hard for me to reconcile how God is perfectly merciful *and* perfectly just at the same time. This tension has the potential to distract us from a core truth about God: He is perfectly just and merciful, all at the same time. That's why he's God and we are not.

Notice with me how God describes the tension between mercy and justice:

> [6] "The LORD, the LORD,
>
> a God merciful and gracious,
>
> slow to anger,
>
> and abounding in steadfast love and faithfulness,
>
> [7] keeping steadfast love for the thousandth generation,
>
> forgiving iniquity and transgression and sin,
>
> yet by no means clearing the guilty,
>
> but visiting the iniquity of the parents
>
> upon the children
>
> and the children's children,
>
> to the third and the fourth generation."
>
> EXODUS 34:6-7

3. **According to Exodus 34:7, how many generations experience the consequences of their parents' sin? And how many generations experience God's steadfast love?**

4. What do you think is God's point in the comparison?

God allows us to experience the consequences of our mistakes, and sometimes that means the people in our lives, even people who are generations removed from our screwups, also feel the impact of our decisions. But the endurance of consequences pales in comparison to the exponential impact of God's steadfast love, which carries on to the thousandth generation. God's loyal love outlasts the consequences of our sin.

5. What is one consequence you are living through? Is it a consequence of something you've done or something done to you?

6. How is God's steadfast love encouraging you?

An important part of understanding the meaning of a Bible passage is getting a sense of its place in the broader storyline of Scripture. When we make connections between different parts of the Bible, we get a glimpse of the unity and cohesion of the Scriptures.

The apostle Paul was arguably one of the greatest leaders who ever lived. Certainly he was one of the most successful ministry leaders, church planters, and missionaries. He wrote several of the New Testament letters that occupy the last half of our Bibles.

In one of his most vulnerable letters, his second letter to the Christians living in Corinth, he admits the highs and lows of serving Jesus in his role. He admits experiencing depression and voices his exasperation that early church leaders were making service to Christ a competition with one another. But he also shares authentically about the joys of living to share the gospel with others.

In 2 Corinthians 3, as he writes about the joys of ministry in the age of the Holy Spirit, Paul brings up the stone tablets we've been studying together in this lesson.

7. **Read 2 Corinthians 3:1–18 and circle any references to Moses and the stone tablets used for the Ten Commandments.**

3 Are we beginning to commend ourselves again? Surely we do not need, as some do, letters of recommendation to you or from you, do we? ² You yourselves are our letter, written on our hearts, to be known and read by all; ³ and you show that you are a letter of Christ, prepared by us, written not with ink but with the Spirit of the living God, not on tablets of stone but on tablets of human hearts.

⁴ Such is the confidence that we have through Christ toward God.
⁵ Not that we are competent of ourselves to claim anything as coming from us; our competence is from God, ⁶ who has made us competent to be ministers of a new covenant, not of letter but of spirit; for the letter kills, but the Spirit gives life.

⁷ Now if the ministry of death, chiseled in letters on stone tablets, came in glory so that the people of Israel could not gaze at Moses' face because of the glory of his face, a glory now set aside, ⁸ how much more will the ministry of the Spirit come in glory? ⁹ For if there was glory in the ministry of condemnation, much more does the ministry of justification abound in glory! ¹⁰ Indeed, what once had glory has lost its glory because of the greater glory; ¹¹ for if what was set aside came through glory, much more has the permanent come in glory!

¹² Since, then, we have such a hope, we act with great boldness, ¹³ not like Moses, who put a veil over his face to keep the people of Israel from gazing at the end of the glory that was being set aside. ¹⁴ But their minds were hardened. Indeed, to this very day, when they hear the reading of the old covenant, that same veil is still there, since only in Christ is it set aside. ¹⁵ Indeed, to this very day whenever Moses is read, a veil lies over their minds; ¹⁶ but when one turns to the Lord, the veil is removed. ¹⁷ Now the Lord is the Spirit, and where the Spirit of the Lord is, there is freedom. ¹⁸ And all of us, with unveiled faces, seeing the glory of the Lord as though reflected in a mirror, are being transformed into the same image from one degree of glory to another; for this comes from the Lord, the Spirit.

2 CORINTHIANS 3:1-18

Moses and the Israelites had only the stone tablets to reference God's directions, but you and I have access to the Holy Spirit. We don't need stone tablets anymore. God writes truth on our hearts through his Holy Spirit.

•   •   •

Let's check back in on our Stones Storyline.

THE STONES STORYLINE OF SCRIPTURE

Bedrock Scripture(s)	Stone Imagery	God's Faithfulness
bedrock of Jacob (Genesis 28, 35)	stone pillow and pillars of stone (altars)	God is faithful to be with us always.
bedrock of Moses (Exodus 34)	two stone tablets	God is faithful to love us no matter what.
bedrock of Joshua (Joshua 4)	stones of remembrance	God is faithful to help us make progress.
bedrock of Jesus (Matthew 27–28)	the stone that was rolled away from Jesus' empty tomb	God is faithful to conquer sin and death.
bedrock of the church (1 Peter 2)	the Living Stone and living stones	God is faithful to make us living stones.

God's Encouragement	God's Transforming Power	Jesus' Fulfillment of the Stones
"I am with you" (Genesis 28:15).	God opens up a path from heaven to earth to be with Jacob.	Jesus tells his disciples, "I am with you always, to the end of the age" (Matthew 28:20).
"The Lord . . . abounding in steadfast love and faithfulness, keeping steadfast love for the thousandth generation" (Exodus 34:6–7).	God keeps his covenant with us even when we are unfaithful.	Paul says that because of Jesus, "you are a letter of Christ . . . written . . . not on tablets of stone but on tablets of human hearts" (2 Corinthians 3:3).
"Let your children know . . . so that all the peoples of the earth may know that the hand of the Lord is mighty, and so that you may fear the Lord your God forever" (Joshua 4:22, 24).	God parts the Jordan River and leads the Israelites across.	Jesus is the new Joshua who fulfills the law of Moses.
"Do not be afraid" (Matthew 28:10).	God's angel rolls away the stone.	Jesus is "the resurrection and the life" (John 11:25).
"Now you are God's people" (1 Peter 2:10).	God transforms us into his witnesses.	Jesus is the Living Stone, the ultimate witness of God's power and grace.

1. Where do you need to be reminded of God's past faithfulness right now? How can you remind yourself of his faithfulness in what you're facing this week?

2. What did you learn about God's character in this lesson?

3. How should these truths shape your faith community and change you?

RESPONDING

The purpose of Bible study is to help you become more Christlike; that's why part 4 will include journaling space for your reflection on and responses to the content and a blank checklist for actionable next steps. You'll be able to process what you're learning so that you can live out the concepts and pursue Christlikeness. Part 4 will enable you to answer the questions *What truths is this passage teaching?* and *How do I apply this to my life?*

IN 2009 I TOOK A LIFE-ALTERING SEMINARY CLASS with Dr. Glenn Kreider. We were supposed to be learning about eschatology, the study of the end times. I acquired plenty of knowledge about the subject matter. But I internalized something even more valuable: God's *steadfast* love. Before this class I had really struggled to comprehend or accept that God's love was free, undeserved, and unearned—let alone that God's love for me, and for you, would never change.

But I know this now: *God loves us no matter what.* God's love for you is loyal, faithful, devoted, kind, and unchanging.

I still catch myself trying to earn God's love or prove to him I'm worthy of it in the first place. What a waste of my time. Whether you are struggling to accept God's steadfast love or convicted that you need to share it with others, here are two benefits of God's steadfast love for you.

1. GOD FORGIVES YOU BECAUSE OF HIS STEADFAST LOVE.

God's forgiveness doesn't negate consequences. When you and I mess up, consequences are a natural part of our emotions, experiences, and relationships. And the severity of the consequences and the impact they have on those around us can be long-lasting. But God is faithful to forgive us. In 1 John 1:9 we read that if we confess our sins, God is faithful and just to forgive us. Let's be the kind of Christians regularly confessing our sins and always open to receiving God's forgiveness.

But don't miss one really important point: God forgives you *because of* his steadfast love. God is love and can't be anything else. Love is in his DNA. He generously pardons our sins not because of our effort but *from a place of love*. Learn from my mistakes. Sometimes I wonder—even as I mentally acknowledge God's love and forgiveness—if I'm on some sliding scale with Jesus. Maybe there is an extra level of forgiveness that I've yet to unlock. God's Word reveals that something different is true. Jesus' capacity to forgive is not based on my abilities or lack thereof. His unyielding love is his motivation.

2. GOD IS PATIENT WITH YOU BECAUSE OF HIS STEADFAST LOVE.

I have a dear friend who grew up in a terribly abusive home. He never knew what awaited him when he walked through the door. His mother was erratic, demeaning, and unpredictable in her abuse. He's mentioned to me that he was constantly questioning his mother's patience. When she didn't jump down his throat or punish him disproportionally to his mistakes, he anticipated that the blowback would come later. Her patience wasn't really patience at all. It would soon be payback.

My friend's childhood trauma skewed his view of God's patience. He's shared with me that for a long time he didn't feel as though he could trust that God was patient. Even after he accepted Christ and slowly unraveled the knots created by his mother's abuse, he was still uneasy about God's generous patience. My friend has worked so hard to unlearn the lessons his mother taught him. Instead, he's applied himself to studying the Scriptures for truth. If he were the one writing this study, he'd tell you that God's patience isn't a trick. God is not secretly waiting to pounce on your insecurities and screwups. Your loving Father waits with open arms to bundle you up in his love. His patience sends him running toward his sons and daughters with the same exuberance shown by the father of the Prodigal Son. How can this be? God's patience for you is supernatural and originates in his character—love.

Use this journaling space to process what you are learning.

Ask yourself how these truths impact your relationship with God and with others.

What is the Holy Spirit bringing to your mind as actionable next steps in your faith journey?

-

-

-

YOUR PROGRESS COMES FROM GOD'S POWER

**BEDROCK OF JOSHUA:
WHERE THE ISRAELITES CROSS THE JORDAN RIVER**

SCRIPTURE: JOSHUA 4

PART 1

CONTEXT

Before you begin your study, we will start with the context of the story we are about to read together: the setting, both cultural and historical; the people involved; and where our passage fits in the larger setting of Scripture. All these things help us make sense of what we're reading. Understanding the context of a Bible story is fundamental to reading Scripture well. Getting your bearings before you read will enable you to answer the question *What am I about to read?*

MOSES WAS ISRAEL'S MOST PROMINENT LEADER, but he wasn't perfect. In fact, his leadership failures kept him from entering the Promised Land. Nevertheless, he was a towering figure in Israel's history. He was rescued as an infant and later became the rescuer of a nation. He was the voice of truth to power in Egypt, the man leading the charge to cross the Red Sea, and the compassionate leader in the wilderness wanderings. When Moses threatened Pharoah, his words carried weight. When Moses threw his staff to the ground, miracles happened. When Moses struck a rock, water came pouring out. My point being— Moses' shoes would have been hard to fill.

In God's providence, Moses' successor, Joshua, had been by Moses' side as his assistant during several transformative moments in Israel's history. Joshua had had

Joshua begins his ministry alongside Moses and stands with him at significant events in Israel's exodus and wilderness experience (Exod 17:8-15; 32:17-18; 33:7-11; Num 13–14). He is commissioned by Moses as his successor (Deut 31:1-13) and this is affirmed by God (Josh 1:1-9). Throughout the book, Joshua takes up Moses' ministry and, in the end, his faithful service is recognized in the title ascribed to him: the "servant of the LORD" (24:29).[1]

Lissa M. Wray Beal, *Joshua* (The Story of God Bible Commentary)

a front-row seat to Moses' brilliance, obedience, and failures. All these learning opportunities served as the education Joshua needed to lead.

Joshua assumed his leadership role under a lot of pressure. Soon after the Moses/Joshua baton-passing ceremony, God reprimanded Moses, saying that he would see the Promised Land but not enter it (Deuteronomy 34:4). Imagine with me that you are taking on a new leadership role as the CEO of a company, and during your introduction to the team, the company owner points out all the unrealized potential of the previous CEO. What a tremendous amount of pressure to inherit! Moses had been an amazing leader, but he was also an enduring example of what happens when you don't finish well.

Maybe this is why Joshua's book in the Old Testament repeats reminders from God to not be afraid or discouraged but to be strong and courageous (Joshua 1:6, 7, 9, 18). Do you need to hear that today? If you have been overcome by fear or discouraged into defeat, stand strong and persevere in courage. Just as God was with Moses and Joshua, he will accompany you as you lead at home, work, and church.

If you've ever served in ministry leadership, you know what it is to see the underbelly of ministry. You see hardships up close. Fear and disappointment have a way of overshadowing hope and conviction when you watch the failures of key leaders in such proximity. Joshua understood what it's like. He was close enough to Moses' failures to fear they would fate his own future.

Like those of Jacob and Moses, Joshua's storyline is stacked with stone imagery:

- *Joshua 4*: Joshua instructs the Israelites crossing the Jordan River to build a memorial of stones so that the nation and all the generations to come will know and trust God as their Rescuer (Joshua 4:20-24).

- *Joshua 8*: Joshua renews the Mosaic covenant with God by writing a copy of God's law on new stones (Joshua 8:32).

- *Joshua 24*: In Joshua's final speech as the leader of Israel, he sets up a large stone under an oak tree to serve as a witness to the renewed covenant God has with his people (Joshua 24:25-27). It is a sacred echo of God's renewed covenant with Jacob in Genesis 35.

Joshua begins his leadership journey with a tremendous amount of apprehension. But God keeps calming his fears with encouraging words and powerful actions. In many ways, Joshua's personal insecurities represent the macro-level insecurities of the nation of Israel. The book of Joshua isn't just about him overcoming *his* fears—it is also a summary of the nation of Israel entering the Promised Land and making progress as a nation.

What you are about to read is an account from Joshua's life in which the Israelites cross over the Jordan River in the same way a previous generation crossed over the Red Sea with Moses. You're going to see progress. And I want to remind you that progress often feels like two steps forward and one step back. Even though you are inching forward, the backward movement can overshadow the fact that you're making headway.

You're also going to see that progress into God's promises is a process. And you're going to see that progress is not about the pathways we route for ourselves but about God's power to make seas into highways. Cosmic water parting isn't the only way God helps us gain new ground, but he's really practiced at it. And that's good news. I have a lot of seemingly impossible things to cross over in my life, and I bet you do too.

Together, we're going to see that progress comes from God's power, not our own.

1. **PERSONAL CONTEXT: What is going on in your life right now that might impact how you understand this Bible story?**

2. **SPIRITUAL CONTEXT: If you've never studied this Bible story before, what piques your curiosity? If you've studied this passage before, what impressions and insights do you recall? What problems or concerns might you have with the passage?**

SEEING

Seeing the text is vital if we want the heart of the Scripture passage to sink in. We read slowly and intentionally through the text with the context in mind. As we practice close, thoughtful reading of Scripture, we pick up on phrases, implications, and meanings we might otherwise have missed. Part 2 includes close Scripture reading and observation questions to empower you to answer the question *What is the story saying?*

1. **Read Joshua 4:1–24 and draw an arrow underneath any descriptions of movement (up, down, forward, backward).**

4 When the entire nation had finished crossing over the Jordan, the LORD said to Joshua: ² "Select twelve men from the people, one from each tribe, ³ and command them, 'Take twelve stones from here out of the middle of the Jordan, from the place where the priests' feet stood, carry them over with you, and lay them down in the place where you camp tonight.'" ⁴ Then Joshua summoned the twelve men from the Israelites, whom he had appointed, one from each tribe. ⁵ Joshua said to them, "Pass on before the ark of the LORD your God into the middle of the Jordan, and each of you take up a stone on his shoulder, one for each of the tribes of the Israelites, ⁶ so that this may be a sign among you. When your children ask in time to come, 'What do those stones mean to you?' ⁷ then you shall tell them that the waters of the Jordan were cut off in front of the ark of the covenant of the LORD. When it crossed over the Jordan, the waters of the Jordan were cut off. So these stones shall be to the Israelites a memorial forever."

⁸ The Israelites did as Joshua commanded. They took up twelve stones out of the middle of the Jordan, according to the number of the tribes of the Israelites, as the LORD told Joshua, carried them over with them to the place where they camped, and laid them down there. ⁹ (Joshua set up twelve stones in the middle of the Jordan, in the place where the feet of the priests bearing the ark of the covenant had stood; and they are there to this day.)

¹⁰ The priests who bore the ark remained standing in the middle of the Jordan, until everything was finished that the LORD commanded Joshua to tell the people, according to all that Moses had commanded Joshua. The people crossed over in haste. ¹¹ As soon as all the people had finished crossing over, the ark of the LORD, and the priests, crossed over in front of the people. ¹² The Reubenites, the Gadites, and the half-tribe of Manasseh crossed over armed before the Israelites, as Moses had ordered them. ¹³ About forty thousand armed for war crossed over before the LORD to the plains of Jericho for battle.

¹⁴ On that day the LORD exalted Joshua in the sight of all Israel; and they stood in awe of him, as they had stood in awe of Moses, all the days of his life.

¹⁵ The LORD said to Joshua, ¹⁶ "Command the priests who bear the ark of the covenant, to come up out of the Jordan." ¹⁷ Joshua therefore commanded the priests, "Come up out of the Jordan." ¹⁸ When the priests bearing the ark of the covenant of the LORD came up from the middle of the Jordan, and the soles of the priests' feet touched dry ground, the waters of the Jordan returned to their place and overflowed all its banks, as before.

¹⁹ The people came up out of the Jordan on the tenth day of the first month, and they camped in Gilgal on the east border of Jericho. ²⁰ Those twelve stones, which they had taken out of the Jordan, Joshua set up in Gilgal, ²¹ saying to the Israelites, "When your children ask their parents in time to come, 'What do these stones mean?' ²² then you shall let your children know, 'Israel crossed over the Jordan here on dry ground.' ²³ For the LORD your God dried up the waters of the Jordan for you until you crossed over, as the LORD your God did to the Red Sea, which he dried up for us until we crossed over, ²⁴ so that all the peoples of the earth may know that the hand of the LORD is mighty, and so that you may fear the LORD your God forever."

JOSHUA 4:1-24

2. List all the reasons you can imagine that moving these rocks would be a challenge.

Despite Joshua's central role, the overwhelming message of the book is that the conquest is God's victory. Joshua's obedience enables him to be God's rightful leader, but God is the divine warrior and architect of the victory (and sometimes the defeat) of the Hebrews.[2]

Amy C. Cottrill, "Joshua," in *Women's Bible Commentary*

During the global pandemic, my family joined many Americans in making some backyard improvements because it was our only place of escape for months. We severely overestimated our ability to follow YouTube instructions in building a patio, though. It was something of a disaster. We didn't think through the logistics of moving the building materials in and out of our backyard or consider how many days the project would take to complete. I imagine the Israelites' endeavor to move rocks from the Jordan riverbed to their camp involved much more work than Joshua describes in the Bible.

3. **Joshua 4:6-7 tells us what the twelve stones represent. Write out what Scripture says about this memorial.**

4. **Kids ask a lot of questions. Notice with me that the Lord anticipates that God's people will get questions from their kids concerning this stone memorial. Based on Joshua 4:6-7, what questions would the kids of Israel ask?**

5. Joshua 4:13 mentions the number of people equipped for war who crossed over the Jordan River. What types of challenges would God's people face trying to move so many people across the riverbed of the Jordan?

I wish the Scriptures gave us more details on the timeline for the Jordan crossing because I have so many unanswered questions about the experience. What I know for sure is that group outings always take longer than planned.

6. Joshua 4:22 offers the Israelite parents a script to use to answer their children when they asked about the meaning of the stone memorial in Gilgal. In your own words, paraphrase how you would tell children what the stone memorial meant to you and to the nation of Israel.

7. What other cosmic water parting is mentioned in Joshua 4:23?

8. **What two things will people learn if they are told about the Jordan-crossing memorial stones (Joshua 4:24)? List both below.**

1.

2.

To know that the Lord is mighty would have been an important lesson for the Israelites because the rest of the book of Joshua details the Canaanite conquest. Battle after battle, Joshua's army succeeds in their fights, but not without severe hardships. Every single person who crossed the Jordan River would need to remember what God did to part the waters and guide the people across to safety. And they would need hope of progress when new challenges confronted them at every turn.

PART 3

UNDERSTANDING

Now that we've finished a close reading of the Scriptures, we're going to spend some time on interpretation: doing our best to understand what God was saying to the original audience and what he's teaching us through the process. But to do so, we need to learn his ways and consider how God's Word would have been understood by the original audience before applying the same truths to our own lives. "Scripture interpretation" may sound a little stuffy, but understanding what God means to communicate to us in the Bible is crucial to enjoying a close relationship with Jesus. Part 3 will enable you to answer the question *What does it mean?*

MY SON, CALEB, started a rock collection. Our family doesn't travel often, but when we do, we're intentional about finding a small rock (or something of that size) to memorialize the trip. His jar full of rocks from Colorado, arrowheads from New Mexico, and pebbles from Branson, Missouri, is what he wants to show our dinner guests. Although he doesn't know much about the type of rocks or items he's collected, he always brings up the same fun stories about the trips represented by each piece in his collection.

The Armstrongs' batch of rocks sends us, and all our dinner guests, down memory lane to appreciate and relive meaningful moments in our life as a family. I'm certain the stone memorial served the same purpose for the Israelites who had crossed the Jordan River. Out of the corners of their eyes, they would get a glimpse of the pile of stones and feel once again the riverbed of the Jordan beneath their feet—and the progress of their people—in their spirits.

1. How would the story of the Jordan crossing encourage the children of Israel? How does it encourage you?

2. How would this story build on the story of the Red Sea crossing?

If I had been one of the Israelites who crossed the Jordan River, I think most of my time spent in the procession would have been occupied with thoughts of the Red Sea crossing. I would have been connecting, comparing, and contrasting the events in my head.

3. What do you think the Israelites may have been connecting, comparing, or contrasting in their heads? Write two examples.

   •

   •

4. Beyond what Joshua told them to share, what do you imagine the Israelite parents would say to their kids about God and his cosmic water partings?

My son, Caleb, wouldn't have been satisfied with the script Joshua gave the Israelites. He would be asking me about the mechanics of the water crossing, where the memorial site stands today, and if it is something that will be present in heaven. Basically, my kid asks me the hardest questions that I almost never have answers to. But if I'd been a parent or mentor during the time of Joshua's leadership, I think I would have made sure to share with Caleb that more impossibilities were going to fill our future. That when it came time to witness the miraculous, our mighty God would make a way for us when there seemed to be no way forward.

5. This was Joshua's first big step of faith without Moses by his side. What do you think Joshua was processing during the procession across the Jordan River?

Was Joshua dealing with imposter syndrome? Did he wish he could turn back time and reject God's calling to lead the nation of Israel? Was he exuberant and dancing across that riverbed? Was he talking the whole time and encouraging the many thousands of people stomping across the river's empty bed? Or was he pensive and deep in thought, pondering the consistency of God? We won't know until glory, but for now we can safely assume that Joshua had Moses in mind as he followed in his footsteps.

6. **How do people act when they're trying to live up to their potential? How do you act when you're trying to live up to your potential?**

7. **Why do you think progress across the Jordan River would have meant so much to the Israelites? What connection would the Red Sea generation be processing as they crossed the Jordan River?**

Forging ahead, across the Jordan River, would have potentially been the single most defining moment in the lives of those who made the journey. But this historic moment would have also been a metaphor for God's unchanging covenant to be with his people and see them through the wilderness wandering to the Promised Land.

8. In what tangible ways do you build your faith? Check all that apply, or fill in the blank at the end.

☐ I take pictures of special moments in my faith.

☐ I collect things that remind me of my faith.

☐ I display verses around my home to remember God's faithfulness.

☐ My desk is full of tangible expressions of my faith.

☐ I create playlists of songs to listen to that can help build my faith.

☐ I journal about my faith.

☐ I wear jewelry to commemorate special moments in my faith life.

☐ I take trips to learn more about my faith.

☐ _____.

Tangible resources are an inextricable part of building an intangible faith. Faith solidifies as we remind ourselves, remember, and internalize what God has done and is doing. Whether we take pictures, journal, post verses, or decorate our desks, we are all trying to keep our faith top of mind.

In the same way, Joshua's stones of remembrance were used to build a memorial site, a place where God's people could celebrate and remember. But soon there would come a time when God's people would build their faith not with stones or rocks but with a story of a gravestone being rolled away.

MAKING CONNECTIONS

An important part of understanding the meaning of a Bible passage is getting a sense of its place in the broader storyline of Scripture. When we make connections between different parts of the Bible, we get a glimpse of the unity and cohesion of the Scriptures.

The rest of the stones storyline will focus on Jesus and his church, but before we make that shift, I want to share with you some of Dr. Lissa M. Wray Beal's scholarship on the book of Joshua. Lissa, an Old Testament professor at a seminary in Canada, beautifully synthesizes how Jesus is the ultimate Joshua. She didn't put this information in a chart in her commentary, but I've paraphrased her words about Joshua's connections to Jesus to create a visual representation of her amazing work.[4]

JOSHUA'S CONNECTIONS TO JESUS

Joshua fulfilled Moses' ministry by leading Israel into the Promised Land.	Christ fulfills Moses' ministry as the final covenant mediator and lawgiver.
Joshua was obedient to God.	Christ is obedient to God, even to the point of death.
Joshua meditated on the law day and night.	Christ is the eternal Word, the Word of God.

The progress the Israelites made across the Jordan River into the Promised Land was also progress in God's plan of redemption for our whole world. When Jesus came to earth, his earliest followers noticed how he fulfilled the roles of Moses and Joshua in a new and incomparable way.

Jesus would also experience his own cosmic water parting during his baptism. Like Joshua, he walked into the Jordan River—and came out of it into breakthrough.

9. Read Mark 1:9–11 and circle the word "Jordan."

[9] In those days Jesus came from Nazareth of Galilee and was baptized by John in the Jordan. [10] And just as he was coming up out of the water, he saw the heavens torn apart and the Spirit descending like a dove on him. [11] And a voice came from heaven, "You are my Son, the Beloved; with you I am well pleased."

MARK 1:9-11

* * *

Let's check back in on our Stones Storyline.

THE STONES STORYLINE OF SCRIPTURE

Bedrock Scripture(s)	Stone Imagery	God's Faithfulness
bedrock of Jacob (Genesis 28, 35)	stone pillow and pillars of stone (altars)	God is faithful to be with us always.
bedrock of Moses (Exodus 34)	two stone tablets	God is faithful to love us no matter what.
bedrock of Joshua (Joshua 4)	stones of remembrance	God is faithful to help us make progress.
bedrock of Jesus (Matthew 27–28)	the stone that was rolled away from Jesus' empty tomb	God is faithful to conquer sin and death.
bedrock of the church (1 Peter 2)	the Living Stone and living stones	God is faithful to make us living stones.

God's Encouragement	God's Transforming Power	Jesus' Fulfillment of the Stones
"I am with you" (Genesis 28:15).	God opens up a path from heaven to earth to be with Jacob.	Jesus tells his disciples, "I am with you always, to the end of the age" (Matthew 28:20).
"The LORD . . . abounding in steadfast love and faithfulness, keeping steadfast love for the thousandth generation" (Exodus 34:6–7).	God keeps his covenant with us even when we are unfaithful.	Paul says that because of Jesus, "you are a letter of Christ . . . written . . . not on tablets of stone but on tablets of human hearts" (2 Corinthians 3:3).
"Let your children know . . . so that all the peoples of the earth may know that the hand of the LORD is mighty, and so that you may fear the LORD your God forever" (Joshua 4:22, 24).	God parts the Jordan River and leads the Israelites across.	Jesus is the new Joshua who fulfills the law of Moses.
"Do not be afraid" (Matthew 28:10).	God's angel rolls away the stone.	Jesus is "the resurrection and the life" (John 11:25).
"Now you are God's people" (1 Peter 2:10).	God transforms us into his witnesses.	Jesus is the Living Stone, the ultimate witness of God's power and grace.

1. Where do you need to be reminded of God's past faithfulness right now? How can you remind yourself of his faithfulness in what you're facing this week?

2. What did you learn about God's character in this lesson?

3. How should these truths shape your faith community and change you?

RESPONDING

The purpose of Bible study is to help you become more Christlike; that's why part 4 will include journaling space for your reflection on and responses to the content and a blank checklist for actionable next steps. You'll be able to process what you're learning so that you can live out the concepts and pursue Christlikeness. Part 4 will enable you to answer the questions *What truths is this passage teaching?* and *How do I apply this to my life?*

ALL I WANTED TO DO was take a little stroll and see the Garden of the Gods. But I made the mistake of not measuring the distance to my destination before I launched into a six-mile trek. I was visiting Colorado Springs and staying at the Glen Eyrie Castle and Conference Center. I'd visited several times before but had never had enough free time to give the Garden of the Gods the attention it deserves. That's why I asked a group of friends to join me on a walk over to the national landmark so I could marvel at the three-hundred-foot sandstone rock formations. And boy, did I miss having my foam roller after that stroll turned into a hike. I was sore for days after walking to and from the Garden of the Gods.

My group of friends and I joked about how none of us knew the history of these rock formations. We were all certain we could do a quick Google search and find our answers, but for the present visit, we surveyed the towering stones hovering above us without knowing how or why they'd found their place in our world.

This is the nature of all good memorials. They are a part of an ongoing story. . . . Ultimately, a powerful memorial enables people to existentially experience the past event so as to live out its demands and implications in the present. This is the power of the stones drawn out of the river. A memorial for future Israelites, they are *aides memoire* that draw people into the story and its present day implications.[5]

Lissa M. Wray Beal, *Joshua* (The Story of God Bible Commentary)

Our trip got me thinking about the people of Israel who lived long after the Jordan River crossing and the formation of the stone memorial. How many times did someone stumble across the memorial site and wonder about its origin story? How many people inquired about the stones of remembrance, only to find answers that would point them to their Creator?

As soon as I landed at home in Dallas, I showed my husband and son pictures from my trip. I couldn't wait to share my adventures with the people closest to me. Then, like any good geriatric millennial, I posted an Instagram reel of my time at the Garden of the Gods. Moments after I posted the pictures, friends reached out to share their own stories of traveling to the Garden of the Gods and how much the rock formations had impacted their own stories.

As we consider the bedrock of Joshua's faith and follow the storyline of stones through the Scriptures, I want to challenge us to keep in mind what God did for Joshua and the Israelites in light of our own faith journeys. Here's what I want you to remember.

1. REMEMBER THAT YOUR PROGRESS COMES FROM GOD'S PRESENCE.

We are a culture zeroed in on leadership pathways and career advancement. It's not enough to start something—we've got to scale it. *Planted a church? Great; how big did it grow? How many multisites were replicated? You started a family? When will you have more kids? You got a promotion? What's your end goal?*

I know we're supposed to value the journey and not the destination, but can we be honest with ourselves? Our destinations are important to us. Where we end up takes up more brain space than we want to admit. In short, we are obsessed with progress. As a result, progress becomes our focus. And I'm concerned that we—myself included—start to confuse who's catapulting us forward in life. Yes, we participate with God in his work, but *our progress comes from God's presence in our lives.*

And the kind of progress I'm talking about is far more significant than where your job will take you. I mean the progress of breaking generational strongholds in your family, the progress of reframing your low view of self to embrace your worthiness as an image bearer of God. You and I can't experience freedom from sin without God's nearness. This should be a huge relief to any of us trying to create forward momentum on our own.

As we move into the next phase of our spiritual journey, let's recognize who's guiding us and accompanying us in our progress.

2. REMEMBER TO MEMORIALIZE YOUR PROGRESS SO YOU WON'T FORGET.

Caleb needs his rock collection, I need my Instagram reels, and the Israelites needed their stone memorial to remember God's favor and faithfulness. We don't just have short memories—we have selective ones. When I feel sad about my life, my first response is to rewrite history. I'll start by taking God's powerful actions in my life up till this point and minimizing them. Sometimes I'll delete progress from the storyline altogether.

I end up retelling stories as void of hope when the truth is that God was working the whole time. God was moving me forward and caring for me every two steps forward and one step back. That's why you and I have to memorialize our progress. If we don't, we're likely to forget all the innumerable ways he has shown up for us and proved himself mighty, trustworthy, and caring. Frame the pictures, post the verses, fill up pages with journal notes. Whatever you do to remember, stay at it. Memorialize your progress. The same God who parted the waters is going to make a way for you to have a bright future.

3. REMEMBER TO SHARE YOUR MEMORIES SO THE NEXT GENERATION HOPES FOR PROGRESS.

Caleb's rocks are not just for his own enjoyment; they're a conversation catalyst to spread joy and happiness. When he shares about our family's adventures, smiles light up all over the room as a new group of people hears for the first time the stories of our past. My Instagram reels aren't just a form of self-expression; they're also an invitation to create community around shared experiences. The Jordan-crossing memorial was not just a pile of rocks for Joshua's followers; it was an expression of faith that is still impacting our lives thousands of years later. My point being: The elements of your story are not just for your own benefit.

Your memories of God's power in your life could be what the next generation needs to hear. I'll be so bold as to say that I *know* it's what they need to hear. Every generation behind you is wondering if God is going to come through for them. Every single Christ follower taking their place in our world desperately needs hope—and your stories will be the delivery mechanism.

Many of us respond to invitations to share our testimonies with hesitation. *What will people think? Why is my story compelling? Isn't there a "better" story to be shared?* But the truth is that we need you to share *your story* of progress. Because what you are really doing is sharing how God powerfully moved through your life to bring you to this point. You're here. God did that. You're going to carry on because God is with you. What if your testimony is the tipping point to stabilize someone else's unbalanced faith? Tip the scales. Let's share with anyone who will listen that our God parted the waters of our lives and brought us safely to the other side.

Use this journaling space to process what you are learning.

Ask yourself how these truths impact your relationship with God and with others.

What is the Holy Spirit bringing to your mind as actionable next steps in your faith journey?

-

-

-

LESSON FOUR

YOUR RESCUE COMES FROM JESUS' RESURRECTION

**BEDROCK OF JESUS:
WHERE THE STONE IS ROLLED AWAY FROM JESUS' EMPTY TOMB**

SCRIPTURE: MATTHEW 27–28

PART 1

CONTEXT

Before you begin your study, we will start with the context of the story we are
about to read together: the setting, both cultural and historical; the people
involved; and where our passage fits in the larger setting of Scripture. All
these things help us make sense of what we're reading. Understanding the
context of a Bible story is fundamental to reading Scripture well. Getting
your bearings before you read will enable you to answer the question *What
am I about to read?*

AGAINST MY BETTER JUDGMENT, I've seen a lot of movies starring
Dwayne "The Rock" Johnson. Because marriage. Aaron's a big fan and has been
since Dwayne's football and wrestling days. To Aaron's credit, and with appreciation for The Rock's talent, his movies do have happy endings, and I appreciate that.

Rolling Stone published a 2018 article titled "The Pain and the Passion That
Fuel the Rock" to promote one of his movie releases. I scrolled all the way to
the end of the online article because I was surprised by something. Many of the
people closest to The Rock give him credit for a big heart. And it seems as though
his big heart is a result of his surviving terrible hardships and setbacks.

The *Rolling Stone* reporter crafted a compelling story and made sure to give
The Rock's new movie a plug. But I couldn't help but notice that all anyone
wanted to talk about when it came to The Rock was his resilience *and* that he
was a wonderful father. No wonder most of his films feature a tough-but-tender
guy overcoming the odds.

In this lesson, we're going to explore a different kind of rolling stone. It's one that can be the reason you and I always get back up after a hard knock. And we're going to talk about a different man who's also called the Rock. Someone who's not just a persona with a strong brand but an enduring person who has the power to conquer death. And we're going to find that Matthew's historical reporting shares something in common with that *Rolling Stone* article: an unexpected theme. You see, Jesus talked a lot about stones in the Bible.

According to professor and former Bible translator Jordan K. Monson,

> There is one material about which [Jesus] could not stop talking: stone. . . .
>
> He spoke of it constantly, particularly of its use in large building projects: towers, foundations, cornerstones, rocks, walls, millstones, temple stones, and winepresses.
>
> When Jesus reached for a metaphor or symbol, stones and building projects filled his semantic toolbox.[1]

Why? Among many other things, Jesus was a master craftsman, a skilled builder, and likely a stonemason.[2]

Isn't it interesting that Jesus probably spent much of his career hammering, breaking, carrying, and laying stone? The same Jesus who was resurrected and walked out of a rock tomb when a gravestone was rolled away and who replaced the Temple completely? Jesus' life experience layers new meaning on the Bible's words about Christ—he was the stone the builders rejected (Psalm 118:22; Matthew 21:42; Mark 12:10; Luke 20:17; Acts 4:11; 1 Peter 2:6-7).

Before we dive into the bedrock of Jesus, I want you to see how the stones storyline develops through Jesus' life and preaching ministry in Matthew's Gospel account.

- *Matthew 4*: The enemy tests Jesus' allegiance to God when he dares Jesus to command stones to become bread (Matthew 4:3). Maybe the enemy is alluding to Jesus' daily grind—stonework.

- *Matthew 7*: In Jesus' famous Sermon on the Mount, he challenges his listeners to build their faith on him because he is the Rock. How does he illustrate his message? He teaches a parable about two different stone foundations. Jesus says that while some may choose to build their "house" on shifting sand, the wise and enduring will build on rock (Matthew 7:24-27).

- *Matthew 16*: One of Jesus' closest friends, Peter, also happened to be one of the most influential early church leaders. Peter was like you and me—his faith wavered at times, really important times, but he loved and served Jesus with faithfulness too. Peter's given name was Simon, and *Peter* was a nickname from Jesus that meant "rock." Jesus' play on words in his conversation with Peter about the future church hints at Peter's part in the Christian movement (Matthew 16:18).

- *Matthew 21*: Jesus gets close to a fire-and-brimstone sermon in the book of Matthew when he tells a parable about a vineyard owner who punishes wicked tenants with death because they have been stealing his produce and murdering his representatives (Matthew 21:33-44). In Christ's parable, the vineyard owner then replaces the workers with faithful new hires. Matthew tells us explicitly that Jesus is speaking to the chief priests and Pharisees, and his point is that they, as power brokers, are being replaced! Jesus concludes his convicting message with this quote from Psalm 118:22: "The stone that the builders rejected has become the cornerstone" (Matthew 21:42).

- *Matthew 24*: Jesus' stone-cold accusations against his accusers don't stop with threatening words in his sermons. He also predicts the destruction of the Temple, the most precious stone building in existence for ancient Israel. In Matthew 24:2 he says that every single stone in the Temple will come crumbling down to rubble. Only the Chief Cornerstone has the authority to say such things.

You're about to read the last two chapters in Matthew's Gospel. These chapters also happen to include the last few times stone imagery is used in the book.

We're about to enter the story when Jesus' preaching and healing ministry has concluded. Everyone whose power had been threatened by Christ's ministry has successfully plotted to arrest and crucify him. And Jesus is dead.

Everyone who hoped Christ was the Messiah is grieving. The mission they devoted their lives to feels lifeless as a rock.

If you know a thing or two—or three—about grieving, I want you to know that I spent time praying for you. I asked God to hold you tight and tender as you read and study this lesson. If you sense you're somehow off mission in life, work, family, or ministry, notice with me how terribly disoriented Christ's disciples felt after his death. Just when we think a mission is reduced to nothing, God has the power to resurrect our hope and enlarge our vision.

You're about to see that your rescue comes from Jesus' resurrection.

1. **PERSONAL CONTEXT: What is going on in your life right now that might impact how you understand this Bible story?**

2. **SPIRITUAL CONTEXT: If you've never studied this Bible story before, what piques your curiosity? If you've studied this passage before, what impressions and insights do you recall? What problems or concerns might you have with the passage?**

PART 2

SEEING

Seeing the text is vital if we want the heart of the Scripture passage to sink in. We read slowly and intentionally through the text with the context in mind. As we practice close, thoughtful reading of Scripture, we pick up on phrases, implications, and meanings we might otherwise have missed. Part 2 includes close Scripture reading and observation questions to empower you to answer the question *What is the story saying?*

1. **Read Matthew 27:57–28:10 and circle any stone imagery you notice.**

⁵⁷ When it was evening, there came a rich man from Arimathea, named Joseph, who was also a disciple of Jesus. ⁵⁸ He went to Pilate and asked for the body of Jesus; then Pilate ordered it to be given to him. ⁵⁹ So Joseph took the body and wrapped it in a clean linen cloth ⁶⁰ and laid it in his own new tomb, which he had hewn in the rock. He then rolled a great stone to the door of the tomb and went away. ⁶¹ Mary Magdalene and the other Mary were there, sitting opposite the tomb.

⁶² The next day, that is, after the day of Preparation, the chief priests and the Pharisees gathered before Pilate ⁶³ and said, "Sir, we remember what that impostor said while he was still alive, 'After three days I will rise again.' ⁶⁴ Therefore command the tomb to be made secure until the

third day; otherwise his disciples may go and steal him away, and tell the people, 'He has been raised from the dead,' and the last deception would be worse than the first." [65] Pilate said to them, "You have a guard of soldiers; go, make it as secure as you can." [66] So they went with the guard and made the tomb secure by sealing the stone.

28 After the sabbath, as the first day of the week was dawning, Mary Magdalene and the other Mary went to see the tomb. [2] And suddenly there was a great earthquake; for an angel of the Lord, descending from heaven, came and rolled back the stone and sat on it. [3] His appearance was like lightning, and his clothing white as snow. [4] For fear of him the guards shook and became like dead men. [5] But the angel said to the women, "Do not be afraid; I know that you are looking for Jesus who was crucified. [6] He is not here; for he has been raised, as he said. Come, see the place where he lay. [7] Then go quickly and tell his disciples, 'He has been raised from the dead, and indeed he is going ahead of you to Galilee; there you will see him.' This is my message for you." [8] So they left the tomb quickly with fear and great joy, and ran to tell his disciples. [9] Suddenly Jesus met them and said, "Greetings!" And they came to him, took hold of his feet, and worshiped him. [10] Then Jesus said to them, "Do not be afraid; go and tell my brothers to go to Galilee; there they will see me."

MATTHEW 27:57–28:10

2. What do we learn about Joseph of Arimathea from Matthew 27:57-58?

-
-
-
-

Joseph is the kind of man who advocates for his dead friend and uses his power, influence, and material wealth to honor Christ's body. I wish we had more details about his life and faith in Jesus. The little we know about Joseph portrays him as a devoted disciple who's evidencing his faith in Christ even while he is grieving. Not only that, but he also uses new real estate to bury Jesus' body.

3. Describe how Joseph closed Jesus' grave. Why do you think Matthew included this detail in his Gospel account?

If Joseph's tomb was large enough to get Jesus' body inside, the stone rolled to close the tomb must have been large. And I wonder just how loud and dusty closing the tomb would have been. How much commotion did this burial stir?

4. What did Pilate's men do to secure the gravesite of Jesus?

Because I know the end of the story, this failed attempt to secure Jesus' tombstone seems laughable. But given what Pilate, his men, and the Pharisees thought they were up against, their security measures make sense. As we reflect on Christ's miraculous bodily resurrection, I can't help but think about how many futile attempts Jesus' enemies made against his life and against him even after his death. Not one of their efforts had the final word.

5. Matthew must have gotten part of his historical records from interviewing the women who'd set up a vigil at Jesus' tomb. What did they tell Matthew happened before their eyes? What had they been staring at while they waited?

6. How do you think the women processed seeing the stone rolled away by the angel of the Lord? What might they have been saying to one another? What do you imagine they were thinking?

I'm going to need a long sit-down with Mary Magdalene in the new heaven and new earth. She and I need to discuss this moment that Matthew describes. Was she crying uncontrollably? Stunned into silence? Yelping with fear? However that conversation goes down, you can be sure I'm going to ask Mary about the stone. Why did the earthquake cause the guards to fall and not the women? Was her faith shaken as that tomb shook loose?

7. Read Matthew 28:1-20. As you read, circle any mention of the women at the empty tomb and underline any mention of stone imagery.

28 After the Sabbath, at dawn on the first day of the week, Mary Magdalene and the other Mary went to look at the tomb.

² There was a violent earthquake, for an angel of the Lord came down from heaven and, going to the tomb, rolled back the stone and sat on it.

³ His appearance was like lightning, and his clothes were white as snow. ⁴ The guards were so afraid of him that they shook and became like dead men.

⁵ The angel said to the women, "Do not be afraid, for I know that you are looking for Jesus, who was crucified. ⁶ He is not here; he has risen, just as he said. Come and see the place where he lay. ⁷ Then go quickly and tell his disciples: 'He has risen from the dead and is going ahead of you into Galilee. There you will see him.' Now I have told you."

⁸ So the women hurried away from the tomb, afraid yet filled with joy, and ran to tell his disciples. ⁹ Suddenly Jesus met them. "Greetings," he said. They came to him, clasped his feet and worshiped him. ¹⁰ Then Jesus said to them, "Do not be afraid. Go and tell my brothers to go to Galilee; there they will see me."

¹¹ While the women were on their way, some of the guards went into the city and reported to the chief priests everything that had happened. ¹² When the chief priests had met with the elders and devised a plan, they gave the soldiers a large sum of money, ¹³ telling them, "You are to say, 'His disciples came during the night and stole him away while we were asleep.' ¹⁴ If this report gets to the governor, we will satisfy him and keep you out of trouble." ¹⁵ So the soldiers took the money and did as they were instructed. And this story has been widely circulated among the Jews to this very day.

¹⁶ Then the eleven disciples went to Galilee, to the mountain where Jesus had told them to go. ¹⁷ When they saw him, they worshiped him; but some doubted. ¹⁸ Then Jesus came to them and said, "All authority in heaven and on earth has been given to me. ¹⁹ Therefore go and make disciples of all nations, baptizing them in the name of the Father and of the Son and of the Holy Spirit, ²⁰ and teaching them to obey everything I have commanded you. And surely I am with you always, to the very end of the age."

MATTHEW 28:1-20, NIV

8. Write out the last thing Jesus says to his disciples in Matthew 28:20.

9. Write out what God says to Jacob in Genesis 28:15, and note the similarities to Matthew 28:20.

Bible scholar Richard B. Hays has this to say about the parallel: "Jesus now stands in the same role occupied by the Lord God in Jacob's dream."[3]

UNDERSTANDING

Now that we've finished a close reading of the Scriptures, we're going to spend some time on interpretation: doing our best to understand what God was saying to the original audience and what he's teaching us through the process. But to do so, we need to learn his ways and consider how God's Word would have been understood by the original audience before applying the same truths to our own lives. "Scripture interpretation" may sound a little stuffy, but understanding what God means to communicate to us in the Bible is crucial to enjoying a close relationship with Jesus. Part 3 will enable you to answer the question *What does it mean?*

1. **Reread Matthew 27:57–28:20. This time, underline anything that reminds you of Jacob's pillars-of-stone story, circle anything that reminds you of Moses' stone-tablets story, and box anything that reminds you of Joshua's stones-of-remembrance story.**

⁵⁷ When it was evening, there came a rich man from Arimathea, named Joseph, who was also a disciple of Jesus. ⁵⁸ He went to Pilate and asked for the body of Jesus; then Pilate ordered it to be given to him. ⁵⁹ So Joseph took the body and wrapped it in a clean linen cloth ⁶⁰ and laid it in his own new tomb, which he had hewn in the rock. He then rolled a great stone to the door of the tomb and went away. ⁶¹ Mary Magdalene and the other Mary were there, sitting opposite the tomb.

⁶² The next day, that is, after the day of Preparation, the chief priests and the Pharisees gathered before Pilate ⁶³ and said, "Sir, we remember what that impostor said while he was still alive, 'After three days I will rise again.' ⁶⁴ Therefore command the tomb to be made secure until the third day; otherwise his disciples may go and steal him away, and tell the people, 'He has been raised from the dead,' and the last deception would be worse than the first." ⁶⁵ Pilate said to them, "You have a guard of soldiers; go, make it as secure as you can." ⁶⁶ So they went with the guard and made the tomb secure by sealing the stone.

28 After the sabbath, as the first day of the week was dawning, Mary Magdalene and the other Mary went to see the tomb. ² And suddenly there was a great earthquake; for an angel of the Lord, descending from heaven, came and rolled back the stone and sat on it. ³ His appearance was like lightning, and his clothing white as snow. ⁴ For fear of him the guards shook and became like dead men. ⁵ But the angel said to the women, "Do not be afraid; I know that you are looking for Jesus who was crucified. ⁶ He is not here; for he has been raised, as he said. Come, see the place where he lay. ⁷ Then go quickly and tell his disciples, 'He has been raised from the dead, and indeed he is going ahead of you to Galilee; there you will see him.' This is my message for you." ⁸ So they left the tomb quickly with fear and great joy, and ran to tell his disciples. ⁹ Suddenly Jesus met them and said, "Greetings!" And they came to him, took hold of his feet, and worshiped him. ¹⁰ Then Jesus said to them, "Do not be afraid; go and tell my brothers to go to Galilee; there they will see me."

¹¹ While they were going, some of the guard went into the city and told the chief priests everything that had happened. ¹² After the priests had assembled with the elders, they devised a plan to give a large sum of money to the soldiers, ¹³ telling them, "You must say, 'His disciples came by night and stole him away while we were asleep.' ¹⁴ If this comes to the governor's ears, we will satisfy him and keep you out of trouble." ¹⁵ So they

took the money and did as they were directed. And this story is still told among the Jews to this day.

¹⁶ Now the eleven disciples went to Galilee, to the mountain to which Jesus had directed them. ¹⁷ When they saw him, they worshiped him; but some doubted. ¹⁸ And Jesus came and said to them, "All authority in heaven and on earth has been given to me. ¹⁹ Go therefore and make disciples of all nations, baptizing them in the name of the Father and of the Son and of the Holy Spirit, ²⁰ and teaching them to obey everything that I have commanded you. And remember, I am with you always, to the end of the age."

MATTHEW 27:57–28:20

2. **How do you think Joseph's friends reacted to his plan to get Jesus' dead body and bury Jesus in his new tomb?**

☐ They assumed his logic was clouded by grief.

☐ They begged him not to waste his property.

☐ They urged him to stop because it was embarrassing.

☐ They cheered him on to do what he could.

☐ They tried to give him a reality check: *Your Savior is dead.*

3. **How do you respond when your friends make big leaps of faith?**

4. Joseph of Arimathea tried to secure Jesus' tomb with a large stone, and Pilate's men tried to secure Jesus' tomb by sealing the rock. You and I work really hard to create security in our own lives. What does that look like for you?

5. After Jesus' death, his disciples were grieving. List any of the emotions you think they may have been processing in their grief, and then go back and circle any of the emotions you feel when you grieve.

6. Why would it have been significant for first-century Christians to read that Jesus appeared to his female disciples first? Why is this detail significant now, for you?

The women holding vigil at Jesus' tomb were some of his most devoted followers. I for one am glad Matthew included this detail in his retelling of the story. Women were not just serving in the periphery of Christ's ministry. They stayed close and were right in the middle of the action.

7. **What do you think Jesus means when he says he has "all authority" in Matthew 28:18?**

When Jesus says "all authority," I think he means *all*. Jesus had authority over the Romans who were in power. Jesus had authority over the Jews, even if they didn't recognize him as their Messiah. Jesus had authority over the Gentiles of his day. He had authority over his disciples. But also, he rules the whole cosmos. Our world and any world beyond. He is transcendent above everything. His power is absolute and unrivaled.

MAKING CONNECTIONS

An important part of understanding the meaning of a Bible passage is getting a sense of its place in the broader storyline of Scripture. When we make connections between different parts of the Bible, we get a glimpse of the unity and cohesion of the Scriptures.

The stones storyline has been building since we studied Jacob's pillars of stone in Genesis. Now that we've added Moses' stone tablets and Joshua's stones of remembrance, I want us to look back at those familiar stories and notice the narrative elements that create a sacred echo in Matthew's account of Jesus' resurrection.

8. **Match a verse from Matthew 27:57–28:20 (left column) to one of the story elements listed below (right column) by drawing a line between the corresponding passages.**

Matthew 27:59-60: "Joseph took the body and wrapped it in a clean linen cloth and laid it in his own new tomb, which he had hewn in the rock."

Matthew 28:2: "an angel of the Lord, descending from heaven"

Matthew 28:20: "I am with you always, to the end of the age."

Matthew 28:2: "[The angel] came and rolled back the stone and sat on it."

In Jacob's story, "the angels of God were ascending and descending" between heaven and earth (Genesis 28:12).

God said to Jacob, "I am with you and will keep you wherever you go" (Genesis 28:15).

God said to Moses, "While my glory passes by I will put you in a cleft of the rock, and I will cover you with my hand until I have passed by" (Exodus 33:22).

In Joshua's story, the men of Israel moved twelve stones from the Jordan riverbed to a new place (Joshua 4:3).

Jesus is the new and better Jacob, the new and better Moses, and the new and better Joshua. Jesus is the Rescuer we've all needed. His resurrection story echoes all the stories we've studied so far, which is a signal: Jesus came to fulfill the Law and Prophets.

* * *

Let's check back in on our Stones Storyline.

THE STONES STORYLINE OF SCRIPTURE

Bedrock Scripture(s)	Stone Imagery	God's Faithfulness
bedrock of Jacob (Genesis 28, 35)	stone pillow and pillars of stone (altars)	God is faithful to be with us always.
bedrock of Moses (Exodus 34)	two stone tablets	God is faithful to love us no matter what.
bedrock of Joshua (Joshua 4)	stones of remembrance	God is faithful to help us make progress.
bedrock of Jesus (Matthew 27–28)	the stone that was rolled away from Jesus' empty tomb	God is faithful to conquer sin and death.
bedrock of the church (1 Peter 2)	the Living Stone and living stones	God is faithful to make us living stones.

God's Encouragement	God's Transforming Power	Jesus' Fulfillment of the Stones
"I am with you" (Genesis 28:15).	God opens up a path from heaven to earth to be with Jacob.	Jesus tells his disciples, "I am with you always, to the end of the age" (Matthew 28:20).
"The LORD . . . abounding in steadfast love and faithfulness, keeping steadfast love for the thousandth generation" (Exodus 34:6–7).	God keeps his covenant with us even when we are unfaithful.	Paul says that because of Jesus, "you are a letter of Christ . . . written . . . not on tablets of stone but on tablets of human hearts" (2 Corinthians 3:3).
"Let your children know . . . so that all the peoples of the earth may know that the hand of the LORD is mighty, and so that you may fear the LORD your God forever" (Joshua 4:22, 24).	God parts the Jordan River and leads the Israelites across.	Jesus is the new Joshua who fulfills the law of Moses.
"Do not be afraid" (Matthew 28:10).	God's angel rolls away the stone.	Jesus is "the resurrection and the life" (John 11:25).
"Now you are God's people" (1 Peter 2:10).	God transforms us into his witnesses.	Jesus is the Living Stone, the ultimate witness of God's power and grace.

1. Where do you need to be reminded of God's past faithfulness right now? How can you remind yourself of his faithfulness in what you're facing this week?

2. What did you learn about God's character in this lesson?

3. How should these truths shape your faith community and change you?

PART 4

RESPONDING

The purpose of Bible study is to help you become more Christlike; that's why part 4 will include journaling space for your reflection on and responses to the content and a blank checklist for actionable next steps. You'll be able to process what you're learning so that you can live out the concepts and pursue Christlikeness. Part 4 will enable you to answer the questions *What truths is this passage teaching?* and *How do I apply this to my life?*

GOD HAS DONE A MIGHTY WORK of rescue in my life. If you've read some of my other books or Bible studies, you know that the Lord rescued me from an unhealthy desire for achievement. You might also know that God rescued me from falling into a substance-abuse addiction that goes back generations in my family. I'm not throwing in a cute or convenient anecdote here—I genuinely thought I was doomed.

I'm not sure I'd be alive right now if not for Jesus. And I know for a fact that I wouldn't have survived my failures if I were still focused on achievement. The crushing disappointments from my past could have very easily led to my destruction—suicidal ideation runs deep in my family.

Jesus didn't just give my life purpose, although that would be reason enough to love him. And he didn't just save my soul, although he most surely has, and I follow him for it. I have no life without my relationship with Jesus. He is everything to me.

That's why this lesson in particular feels so tender. Jacob's faith becoming his own in lesson one changed me. Moses' advocacy for his people in lesson two changed me. Joshua's progress in lesson three changed me. But the stone rolling away for Jesus' resurrection—I was undone.

I want to share with you two thoughts that the Spirit kept bringing to my mind as I wept over Jesus proving he is the rescue we all need.

1. JESUS' RESURRECTION RESCUES YOU FROM UNENDING GRIEF.

Grief is the least predictable struggle I've had to face. At least with anger, I know what can set me off. With disappointment, I know what's going to hurt my feelings or send me into depression. But grief—she's cruelly surprising. You'll be fine one moment and a mess the next. You'll think you're finally past a deep wound, and grief drudges up the whole history with pangs of pain. If we were together in person, I'd ask you what you are grieving. I have no doubt we could spend hours processing how you are navigating grief, because *we all deal with it.* Sometimes it's the grief of a lost opportunity, a failed relationship, the end of a friendship, the ache of loneliness. Maybe you've lost someone to the tragedy of terminal illness. Whatever it may be, I wish I were with you now to make space for your grief.

Joseph of Arimathea must have been beside himself with grief as he buried his friend Jesus. Joseph really believed that Jesus was the answer to his prayers, the future for his life, the reigning King of Israel, his salvation. And then Jesus was dead in his arms. We can't know how Joseph internalized or expressed his grief. But I would imagine wrapping Jesus' brutalized body with clean linens was an emotionally charged experience.

Mary Magdalene and the other female disciples holding vigil at Jesus' tomb were grieving their leader and healer. He'd rescued Mary from a life of demon possession and set her free to serve in leadership within the Jesus community. And then he was gone. All her hopes and dreams were wrapped up in Christ—but then he was crucified.

One of the points of Jesus' resurrection is that it rescues you and me from unending grief. Grief will always be part of our reality in this life, but in the life to come—*grief be gone!* Done. Zero. Zilch. Take heart: The grief you are dealing with now will not be forever. It has an end date. And in the meantime, your Savior is closer to you in a state of brokenheartedness than ever before. Jesus reserves a special nearness for those of us in a dark night of the soul, the valley of the shadow of death, and the pit of despair.

2. JESUS' RESURRECTION COMMISSIONS YOU TO SERVE UNREACHED PEOPLE.

Imagining the stone being rolled away from Jesus' tomb has my heart racing. I'm envisioning the great rock turning in slow motion like in a triumphal movie scene, and the anticipation of it all makes my heart feel as though it might explode. And then the great commission? It's too much, y'all. Not only did Jesus' resurrection rescue us from sin, death, and unending grief; Jesus' resurrection commissions you and me to serve unreached people.

Jesus dealt with the doubt the disciples were still processing by comforting them with words about his ongoing presence—he'd be with them always, even to the very end of the age. But he also put a calling on their lives as disciples and, in so doing, gave us our calling too. He set us loose to share his love with anyone and everyone.

So, go on then. No matter how grief tattered or doubtful you feel, you are commissioned and empowered to go anyway. Go with the gospel news the way Joseph of Arimathea and Mary Magdalene would have—still processing their grief, still shook from Jesus' resurrection—but *go*. You don't need any more memorial stones! Because the stone has been rolled away, and *the* Rock is alive.

Use this journaling space to process what you are learning.

Ask yourself how these truths impact your relationship with God and with others.

What is the Holy Spirit bringing to your mind as actionable next steps in your faith journey?

-
-
-

YOUR PURPOSE COMES FROM THE CHURCH'S POSITION

BEDROCK OF THE CHURCH:
WHERE PETER CHALLENGES CHRISTIANS TO BE LIKE CHRIST

SCRIPTURE: 1 PETER 2

PART 1

CONTEXT

Before you begin your study, we will start with the context of the story we are about to read together: the setting, both cultural and historical; the people involved; and where our passage fits in the larger setting of Scripture. All these things help us make sense of what we're reading. Understanding the context of a Bible story is fundamental to reading Scripture well. Getting your bearings before you read will enable you to answer the question *What am I about to read?*

MEREDITH KING IS THE BEST LEADER I KNOW. Mutual friends had told me about her exceptional leadership for a long time, but now that she leads me, I can confirm: Her reputation checks out. She's been invested in the **Storyline Bible Studies** since long before there were any words to show for them, and she's been praying for you, the person reading, for months. Her words of affirmation during the writing process are one of the reasons this Bible study is in your hands.

But her reaction to the *Stones* Bible study went far beyond even her support for everything else I was doing. The day I shared with Meredith that I'd be following stone imagery through the Bible, her excitement went to another level.

"Did you know," she asked me, "that a geology class changed my spiritual life?"

Meredith needed two science credits for her liberal arts degree, and when it came time to choose her classes, she opted into one on geology. Meredith has always been fascinated by large rock formations and the stones in creation. I wish you could hear the inflection in her voice when she describes what happened in her heart when she visited Zion National Park in Utah and marveled at the large stone formations. Or the passion with which she retells visiting the Rocky Mountains and being awed by God's genius and enormity.

Her geology class providentially coincided with her desire to know Jesus better. She'd long been a follower of Christ, but this was a time when she needed Jesus in a more tangible, personal way. She started her geology class curious, with anticipation—but what she learned blew her mind. She finished a science class on the earth's physical structures with a B, but she gained a newfound appreciation for God's power, creativity, and character. God, after all, was there before one of the rocks was formed, before any mountain emerged from the earth's crust. And he's the One who set our world into motion.

Meredith's seat, or position, in a geology class clarified her purpose: She wanted to love this awe-inspiring, rock-forming God, and she was called to love others, too. In a similar way, your position in God's Kingdom determines your purpose in life. Together we'll see this truth as we do a deep dive into one of Peter's New Testament letters: 1 Peter.

Peter understood position-determined purpose because he was in Jesus' inner circle as one of the twelve disciples. Theologians N. T. Wright and Michael F. Bird summarize Peter's life this way:

> It was Peter who made the dramatic pronouncement that Jesus was the Messiah. It was also Peter, notoriously, who denied Jesus in the high priest's hall. However, he became a key witness to Jesus' resurrection, not least through a personal meeting with the risen Jesus in which he was restored to his position of leadership.[1]

Peter's status as a close friend and follower of Jesus determined much of his influence in the early church movement. His position in Jesus' inner circle was threatened by his cowardice and denial of Jesus, but Christ lovingly restored Peter to his position as a servant in God's Kingdom—and, in doing so, reaffirmed his

Peter writes to Christians in Asia Minor who are suffering for their faith. He comforts them with reminders of the solid hope for salvation they enjoy because of Christ's death and resurrection and challenges them to maintain the highest standards of holy living as a witness to their persecutors.[2]

D. A. Carson and Douglas J. Moo, *An Introduction to the New Testament*

purpose to go and make disciples. All these life experiences positioned Peter to teach us about being living stones.

Peter's use of the metaphor of stones isn't random: Remember that Jesus gave him the nickname *Peter*, meaning "rock." In one pivotal scene in Peter's life, Jesus tells him he is going to be the bedrock of the church. We can take this to mean many different things, but I want to zero in on one. Peter would be one of the first living stones, showing Christians like you and me how to live into that same calling.

What you are about to read is Peter's first letter to Christians spread throughout Asia Minor. His letter addresses their fears and struggles through persecution, and he comforts them, challenges them, and calms their fears by reminding them that Christ is the Living Stone. The stone was rolled away for him; and we, too, are living stones. We, too, are going to experience a resurrection. Until then, Peter urges Christians to testify to God's mighty acts.

If you feel purposeless or just have nagging concerns that you are not fully embracing your God-given purpose, this lesson is for you. What you are going to see is that you have a position in God's Kingdom—and your position gives you purpose.

1. **PERSONAL CONTEXT: What is going on in your life right now that might impact how you understand this Bible passage?**

2. **SPIRITUAL CONTEXT: If you've never studied this Bible passage before, what piques your curiosity? If you've studied this passage before, what impressions and insights do you recall? What problems or concerns might you have with the passage?**

PART 2

SEEING

Seeing the text is vital if we want the heart of the Scripture passage to sink in. We read slowly and intentionally through the text with the context in mind. As we practice close, thoughtful reading of Scripture, we pick up on phrases, implications, and meanings we might otherwise have missed. Part 2 includes close Scripture reading and observation questions to empower you to answer the question *What is the story saying?*

1. **Read 1 Peter 2:4-10 and underline any stone imagery.**

⁴ Come to him, a living stone, though rejected by mortals yet chosen and precious in God's sight, and ⁵ like living stones, let yourselves be built into a spiritual house, to be a holy priesthood, to offer spiritual sacrifices acceptable to God through Jesus Christ. ⁶ For it stands in scripture:

"See, I am laying in Zion a stone,
　　a cornerstone chosen and precious;
and whoever believes in him will not be put to shame."

⁷ To you then who believe, he is precious; but for those who do not believe,

"The stone that the builders rejected
　　has become the very head of the corner,"

[8] and

> "A stone that makes them stumble,
>> and a rock that makes them fall."

They stumble because they disobey the word, as they were destined to do.
[9] But you are a chosen race, a royal priesthood, a holy nation, God's own people, in order that you may proclaim the mighty acts of him who called you out of darkness into his marvelous light.

> [10] Once you were not a people,
>> but now you are God's people;
> once you had not received mercy,
>> but now you have received mercy.

1 PETER 2:4-10

2. **Peter gives Christians two exhortations in 1 Peter 2:4–5 and then lists three outcomes of the actions he exhorts us to take. List all of them below.**

   Exhortations:

       1.

       2.

In this new identification, Peter does not focus on their individual status, but collectively they are living stones joined together by God through Jesus Christ. Together they represent a spiritual house, wherein they are a holy priesthood, and Jesus Christ stands as the chief cornerstone, holding the entire people in unity with God.[3]

Larry George, "1 Peter," in *True to Our Native Land*

The Holy Rock of Zion was very early understood as the cosmic cornerstone (Isa 28:16; cf. Mt 16:19) which forms the summit of the world-mountain (Ps 61:1c) and which restrains the rising waters of Chaos. With his own hands God set this stone in place (Job 38:6; cf. Pss 78:68; 87:1).[4]

Othmar Keel, *The Symbolism of the Biblical World*

Outcomes:

1.

2.

3.

I find it wildly comforting to know that our first step toward our purpose is to come to Jesus. Peter doesn't tell us to get our act together—he tells us to approach our Savior. God is the One who empowers our lives.

3. How was Jesus "rejected by mortals" (1 Peter 2:4)? List all the forms of rejection you can think of that Jesus experienced.

Jesus was rejected by his ethnic group, the Jews. He was rejected by the religious elite, the Pharisees, Sadducees, and chief priests. And he was rejected by one of his closest friends and ministry partners, Judas. Those are only to name a few. Jesus knew full well what it is like to be denied, abandoned, deserted, and forsaken. To anyone wincing from rejection, your Savior understands what you are going through, and he cares deeply. He cared enough to live through it himself and relate to your pain. And he endured all this rejection so that you and I could have a relationship with God. His rejection is our acceptance.

4. Describe a time when you felt rejected. How did you respond?

5. What is the difference between a stone and a living stone? Or to put it another way, what can a living stone do that a regular stone can't? Brainstorm and make a list below.

Pet rocks have always confused me. They can't move, communicate, grow, or adapt. This is what comes to mind as I consider the difference between a regular ol' rock and a living stone.

6. How does Peter describe the Lord? List all the descriptors you can find in 1 Peter 2.

7. Why do you think Peter names Jesus the Living Stone (1 Peter 2:4)?

8. If you recognize any Old Testament echoes in this passage—any allusions to a story we've already studied (Jacob, Moses, or Joshua)—list what you've noticed.

The first thing that jumped out at me was Peter's encouragement to let ourselves be built into a spiritual house. I thought of Jacob's altar to God—Jacob positioning the stone to make a pillar.

9. Peter describes our position in God's Kingdom three different ways in 1 Peter 2:9. List his descriptors. Beside each point, write whether you believe this about yourself. Why or why not?

Descriptors of Our Position in God's Kingdom	Your Response to Each Descriptor
1.	
2.	
3.	

The hard one for me is *holy*. Theoretically, I understand that I gained Christ's righteousness through his life, death, and resurrection. But practically speaking, I don't feel wholly at ease living into this identity of holiness, even knowing I am chosen by God and set apart to join his royal Kingdom.

The entire list is humbling. None of these things are possible in our own strength. In fact, I would say they sound outrageously undeserved. But that's the point, right? We might view ourselves as dead rocks, but Jesus invites us, through Peter, to live like stones that are alive.

UNDERSTANDING

Now that we've finished a close reading of the Scriptures, we're going to spend some time on interpretation: doing our best to understand what God was saying to the original audience and what he's teaching us through the process. But to do so, we need to learn his ways and consider how God's Word would have been understood by the original audience before applying the same truths to our own lives. "Scripture interpretation" may sound a little stuffy, but understanding what God means to communicate to us in the Bible is crucial to enjoying a close relationship with Jesus. Part 3 will enable you to answer the question *What does it mean?*

ONE OF THE REASONS my friend Meredith is such a great leader is that she models to me the behavior she would like me to emulate. She goes first. This is leadership I can get behind. I know that she isn't going to ask of me something she isn't willing to do herself. Plus she's always quick to admit when she is wrong or that she is still a work in progress. That's why I love following her lead.

I feel similarly about Peter. Peter is one of the leaders we can look to in Scripture who has gone first in our faith. He's lived through a radical conversion himself and watched thousands of others come to faith in Christ. He knows the lows of ministry failures and the highs of being restored. Peter denied Christ when Jesus was looking for his support but also experienced the joys of preaching truth when he knew it wouldn't be well received. He was one of the few people to witness Christ's ministry up close, to experience the pain of Jesus' crucifixion, and to see Jesus resurrected. And Peter was one of the few to hear Jesus' great commission speech and to be present at Pentecost, when the Holy Spirit came on the first Christians.

Knowing a little of his backstory shapes how I understand his writing in 1 Peter. When Peter exhorts Christians to come to the Living Stone and to be living stones, I trust he knows what he's talking about based on his lived experience. Peter knows what persecuted Christians need to hear to be encouraged and to stay the course—which is why he chooses to quote several Old Testament passages in his letter.

1. **Read 1 Peter 2:4-10 and notice the three Old Testament passages quoted. Why do you think Peter chooses these three passages?**

2. **Based on 1 Peter 2:9, what is the church's purpose?**

3. **What is Peter alluding to when he says we have been called out of darkness and into the light (1 Peter 2:9)? What other passages of Scripture come to mind when you think about the darkness/light imagery?**

4. In your own life, how can you proclaim God's mighty acts? List a few ways you could do that practically.

MAKING CONNECTIONS

An important part of understanding the meaning of a Bible passage is getting a sense of its place in the broader storyline of Scripture. When we make connections between different parts of the Bible, we get a glimpse of the unity and cohesion of the Scriptures.

At the end of the Bible's storyline is the book of Revelation. Revelation gives us glimpses into the world to come, the new heaven and earth, when evil will no longer exist. The author of Revelation is the apostle John, one of Jesus' closest friends and a faithful disciple. John is given a vision from God about our future if we are Christ followers: a world without tears and suffering.

Embedded in the imagery John uses to describe our future glory is the culmination of the rock and stone storyline we've been studying together.

5. **Read Revelation 2:17 and circle any stone imagery you see.**

> [17] "Whoever has ears, let them hear what the Spirit says to the churches. To the one who is victorious, I will give some of the hidden manna. I will also give that person a white stone with a new name written on it, known only to the one who receives it."
>
> REVELATION 2:17, NIV

6. Read Revelation 4:1-3 and circle any stone imagery you see.

4 After this I looked, and there before me was a door standing open in heaven. And the voice I had first heard speaking to me like a trumpet said, "Come up here, and I will show you what must take place after this." ² At once I was in the Spirit, and there before me was a throne in heaven with someone sitting on it. ³ And the one who sat there had the appearance of jasper and ruby. A rainbow that shone like an emerald encircled the throne.

REVELATION 4:1-3, NIV

From almost the beginning of history, God's people have been building altars and memorials with rocks and stones to remember God's faithfulness and worship him for his trustworthiness. All the stones laid in formation as symbols of God's presence find their fulfillment, their ultimate destination, in the eternal throne room of heaven. God himself is described as appearing like precious stones.

• • •

Let's check back in on our Stones Storyline.

THE STONES STORYLINE OF SCRIPTURE

Bedrock Scripture(s)	Stone Imagery	God's Faithfulness
bedrock of Jacob (Genesis 28, 35)	stone pillow and pillars of stone (altars)	God is faithful to be with us always.
bedrock of Moses (Exodus 34)	two stone tablets	God is faithful to love us no matter what.
bedrock of Joshua (Joshua 4)	stones of remembrance	God is faithful to help us make progress.
bedrock of Jesus (Matthew 27–28)	the stone that was rolled away from Jesus' empty tomb	God is faithful to conquer sin and death.
bedrock of the church (1 Peter 2)	the Living Stone and living stones	God is faithful to make us living stones.

God's Encouragement	God's Transforming Power	Jesus' Fulfillment of the Stones
"I am with you" (Genesis 28:15).	God opens up a path from heaven to earth to be with Jacob.	Jesus tells his disciples, "I am with you always, to the end of the age" (Matthew 28:20).
"The LORD . . . abounding in steadfast love and faithfulness, keeping steadfast love for the thousandth generation" (Exodus 34:6-7).	God keeps his covenant with us even when we are unfaithful.	Paul says that because of Jesus, "you are a letter of Christ . . . written . . . not on tablets of stone but on tablets of human hearts" (2 Corinthians 3:3).
"Let your children know . . . so that all the peoples of the earth may know that the hand of the LORD is mighty, and so that you may fear the LORD your God forever" (Joshua 4:22, 24).	God parts the Jordan River and leads the Israelites across.	Jesus is the new Joshua who fulfills the law of Moses.
"Do not be afraid" (Matthew 28:10).	God's angel rolls away the stone.	Jesus is "the resurrection and the life" (John 11:25).
"Now you are God's people" (1 Peter 2:10).	God transforms us into his witnesses.	Jesus is the Living Stone, the ultimate witness of God's power and grace.

1. Where do you need to be reminded of God's past faithfulness right now? How can you remind yourself of his faithfulness in what you're facing this week?

2. What did you learn about God's character in this lesson?

3. How should these truths shape your faith community and change you?

RESPONDING

The purpose of Bible study is to help you become more Christlike; that's why part 4 will include journaling space for your reflection on and responses to the content and a blank checklist for actionable next steps. You'll be able to process what you're learning so that you can live out the concepts and pursue Christlikeness. Part 4 will enable you to answer the questions *What truths is this passage teaching?* and *How do I apply this to my life?*

WHEN MEREDITH STEPPED INTO her geology class, she was dealing with some challenging health struggles. As she processed what she was learning about the earth's composition, she was also processing her faith as a disciple of Jesus and trying to find her place in this world. Geology gave Meredith concrete reasons to embrace her position in God's Kingdom and live out her purpose for God's glory.

- *Concrete reason #1*: Long before anyone climbed the Rockies, scaled Kilimanjaro, or photographed the beauty of the Zion formations, God was on his throne. And he'll be there after those mountains are no longer. God is enduring. We can trust that he won't be moved or shaken.

- *Concrete reason #2*: Rock and stone formations, including mountains, are formed over time and under pressure. This process has a lot in common with Christian discipleship. You and I are formed into Christ's likeness over time—and sometimes under pressure, too.

- *Concrete reason #3*: New parts of the earth emerge from underneath, but not before a colossal collision of the earth's tectonic plates, or pieces of the earth's crust. The catastrophic can also create something beautiful.

God is enduring, and in the mystery of his work and ways, beautiful new things are emerging in our lives from some of the hardest things we're facing. The work of discipleship is a long process that sometimes involves being under pressure, but our God will see it through. With that in mind, I want to encourage you to do two things.

1. EMBRACE YOUR POSITION IN GOD'S KINGDOM.

The one true, living God—the God of the universe—chose you. You are his dream come true. He positioned you to be alive now. For this time, in this place, with these people. With great intentionality and insight, God wanted you here, now. If you're anything like me, you wonder, *Why? How?* What I know for sure is that if you put your faith in Christ and follow him, you're mission critical to his Kingdom. So embrace your position. I'll bet you and I both have spent enough time feeling wishy-washy about where we belong and whether we are in the right place in life. I think our time is better spent embracing that we are chosen, royal, and holy in Christ. That we have been called "out of darkness into his marvelous light" (1 Peter 2:9). That we were created with purpose, on purpose, and for a purpose because we are a part of God's amazing Kingdom. Peter puts it this way in 1 Peter 2:10: "Once you were not a people, but now you are God's people."

2. LIVE OUT YOUR PURPOSE FOR GOD'S GLORY.

When Peter challenges the persecuted Christians he addresses in his letter, he says that they need to "proclaim the mighty acts of [God]" (1 Peter 2:9). Namely, that Jesus was resurrected from death, which means that death cannot conquer any who follow him either (1 Peter 1:3-5). By extension, you and I are called to the same thing. We, too, are purposed to be proclaimers of God's might. Now, don't for one minute assume this means we all have to become preachers or pastors. Just the opposite. We need Christ followers in every industry, in every place, to reach everyone with the hope of the Resurrection. How should we go about gospel proclamation? It's going to look different for each of us. We need to contextualize the most effective ways to live out our purpose, but I know for sure it will involve sharing with others this mighty act of God in your life: "Once you had not received mercy, but now you have received mercy" (1 Peter 2:10).

Use this journaling space to process what you are learning.

Ask yourself how these truths impact your relationship with God and with others.

What is the Holy Spirit bringing to your mind as actionable next steps in your faith journey?

-
-
-

As You Go

JACOB, MOSES, AND JOSHUA erected, gathered, and chiseled out rocks to leave lasting reminders of the power and faithfulness of God. But in the new heaven and earth, we won't need these stone memorials. Jesus, the Living Stone, will be seated in the midst of innumerable living stones—you and me and all God's people, who will forever bear witness to the marvelous things he has done.

The stones God's people needed to mark his work have no more use in the new heaven and new earth.

> [18] The wall was made of jasper, and the city of pure gold, as pure as glass. [19] The foundations of the city walls were decorated with every kind of precious stone. The first foundation was jasper, the second sapphire, the third agate, the fourth emerald, [20] the fifth onyx, the sixth ruby, the seventh chrysolite, the eighth beryl, the ninth topaz, the tenth turquoise, the eleventh jacinth, and the twelfth amethyst. [21] The twelve gates were

twelve pearls, each gate made of a single pearl. The great street of the city was of gold, as pure as transparent glass.

²² I did not see a temple in the city, because the Lord God Almighty and the Lamb are its temple.

REVELATION 21:18-22, NIV

The city itself is a memorial. And we are its living stones, the new and eternal remembrance of God's great work among his people, vibrant with the life of the risen Savior.

● ● ●

You did it. You studied the bedrocks of Jacob, Moses, Joshua, Jesus, and the church:

- *Genesis 28, 35*: the bedrock of Jacob, when Jacob's faith became his own;
- *Exodus 34*: the bedrock of Moses, when Moses asked for God's forgiveness;
- *Joshua 4*: the bedrock of Joshua, when the Israelites crossed the Jordan River;
- *Matthew 27–28*: the bedrock of Jesus, when the stone was rolled away from Jesus' empty tomb; and
- *1 Peter 2*: the bedrock of the church, when Peter challenged Christians to be like Christ.

All five bedrock stories share several key elements:

- God is proved faithful to us always,
- God gives us encouragement so that we can make him the Bedrock of our faith,
- God's transforming power changes everything, and
- Jesus fulfills all the stone imagery in his resurrection.

These stand-out elements bring together a cohesive storyline.

THE STONES STORYLINE OF SCRIPTURE

Bedrock Scripture(s)	Stone Imagery	God's Faithfulness
bedrock of Jacob (Genesis 28, 35)	stone pillow and pillars of stone (altars)	God is faithful to be with us always.
bedrock of Moses (Exodus 34)	two stone tablets	God is faithful to love us no matter what.
bedrock of Joshua (Joshua 4)	stones of remembrance	God is faithful to help us make progress.
bedrock of Jesus (Matthew 27–28)	the stone that was rolled away from Jesus' empty tomb	God is faithful to conquer sin and death.
bedrock of the church (1 Peter 2)	the Living Stone and living stones	God is faithful to make us living stones.

God's Encouragement	God's Transforming Power	Jesus' Fulfillment of the Stones
"I am with you" (Genesis 28:15).	God opens up a path from heaven to earth to be with Jacob.	Jesus tells his disciples, "I am with you always, to the end of the age" (Matthew 28:20).
"The LORD . . . abounding in steadfast love and faithfulness, keeping steadfast love for the thousandth generation" (Exodus 34:6-7).	God keeps his covenant with us even when we are unfaithful.	Paul says that because of Jesus, "you are a letter of Christ . . . written . . . not on tablets of stone but on tablets of human hearts" (2 Corinthians 3:3).
"Let your children know . . . so that all the peoples of the earth may know that the hand of the LORD is mighty, and so that you may fear the LORD your God forever" (Joshua 4:22, 24).	God parts the Jordan River and leads the Israelites across.	Jesus is the new Joshua who fulfills the law of Moses.
"Do not be afraid" (Matthew 28:10).	God's angel rolls away the stone.	Jesus is "the resurrection and the life" (John 11:25).
"Now you are God's people" (1 Peter 2:10).	God transforms us into his witnesses.	Jesus is the Living Stone, the ultimate witness of God's power and grace.

With every bedrock story, I hope God reminded you that he is faithful. You can make Jesus the Bedrock of your life—the very foundation of all you are and do. Because Jesus is your Rock of refuge, your sure foundation, your stronghold, your unshakable King.

Now's your time to be a living stone—someone who shows with their life how Jesus changed everything.

PS: I've loved this time with you, and I hope you join me again for another journey in the **Storyline Bible Studies**.

Each **Storyline Bible Study** is five lessons long and can be paired with its thematic partner for a seamless ten-week study. Complement the *Stones* study with

STICKS
ROOTING YOUR FAITH IN GODLY WISDOM
WHEN YOUR DECISIONS MATTER THE MOST

Trees are where God's people have had to make hard choices. And as one of God's preferred symbols in the Bible, trees take on symbolic meaning as places where we can choose to live wisely.

LESSON ONE: Choosing Wisely instead of Taking Matters into Your Own Hands
The Tree of Life and the Tree of the Knowledge of Good and Evil: Where Adam and Eve Listen to the Wrong Voice
GENESIS 2–3

LESSON TWO: Taking Notice When God Is Trying to Get Your Attention
The Burning Bush: Where God Reveals His Identity to Moses
EXODUS 3

LESSON THREE: Branching Out from Your Shady Family Tree
The Messiah Tree: Where God's People Find Hope for the Future
ISAIAH 1, 6, 11, 53

LESSON FOUR: Staying Connected to Jesus for a Fruitful Life
The True Vine, Jesus: Where We Produce Love and Joy
JOHN 15

LESSON FIVE: Reframing Your Perspective with Views from the Treetops
The Tree of Life: Where God's Glory Redeems All Things
REVELATION 22

Learn more at thestorylineproject.com.

CP1843

Storyline Bible Studies

Each study follows people, places, or things throughout the Bible.
This approach allows you to see the cohesive storyline of Scripture
and appreciate the Bible as the literary masterpiece that it is.

**Access free resources to help you teach or
lead a small group at thestorylineproject.com.**

STORYLINE

CP1816

Acknowledgments

WITHOUT MY FAMILY'S SUPPORT, the **Storyline Bible Studies** would just be a dream. I'm exceedingly grateful for a family that prays and cheers for me when I step out to try something new. To my husband, Aaron, son, Caleb, and mom, Noemi: You three sacrificed the most to ensure that I had enough time and space to write. Thank you. And to all my extended family: I know an army of Armstrongs was praying and my family in Austin was cheering me on to the finish line. Thank you.

To my ministry partners at the Polished Network, Integrus Leadership, and Dallas Bible Church: Linking arms with you made this project possible. I love doing Kingdom work with you.

NavPress and Tyndale teams: Thank you for believing in me. You wholeheartedly embraced the concept, and you've made this project better in every way possible. Special thanks to David Zimmerman, my amazing editor Caitlyn Carlson, Elizabeth Schroll, Olivia Eldredge, David Geeslin, and the entire editorial and marketing teams.

Jana Burson: You were the catalyst. Thank you.

Teresa Swanstrom Anderson: Thank you for connecting me with Caitlyn. You'll forever go down in history as the person who made my dreams come true.

All my friends rallied to pray for this project when I was stressed about the deadlines. Thank you. We did it! Without your intercession, these wouldn't be complete. I want to give special thanks to Lee, Sarah, Amy, Amy, Tiffany, and Jenn for holding up my arms to complete the studies.

Resources for Deeper Study

OLD TESTAMENT

Bearing God's Name: Why Sinai Still Matters by Carmen Joy Imes

The Epic of Eden: A Christian Entry into the Old Testament by Sandra L. Richter

NEW TESTAMENT

Echoes of Scripture in the Gospels by Richard B. Hays

The Gospels as Stories: A Narrative Approach to Matthew, Mark, Luke, and John by Jeannine K. Brown

BIBLE STUDY

Commentary on the New Testament Use of the Old Testament, eds. G. K. Beale and D. A. Carson

Dictionary of Biblical Imagery, eds. Leland Ryken, James C. Wilhoit, and Tremper Longman III

The Drama of Scripture: Finding Our Place in the Biblical Story by Craig G. Bartholomew and Michael W. Goheen

How (Not) to Read the Bible: Making Sense of the Anti-Women, Anti-Science, Pro-Violence, Pro-Slavery and Other Crazy Sounding Parts of Scripture by Dan Kimball

How to Read the Bible as Literature . . . and Get More Out of It by Leland Ryken

Literarily: How Understanding Bible Genres Transforms Bible Study by Kristie Anyabwile

The Mission of God: Unlocking the Bible's Grand Narrative by Christopher J. H. Wright

"Reading Scripture as a Coherent Story" by Richard Bauckham, in *The Art of Reading Scripture*, eds. Ellen F. Davis and Richard B. Hays

Reading While Black: African American Biblical Interpretation as an Exercise in Hope by Esau McCaulley

Read the Bible for a Change: Understanding and Responding to God's Word by Ray Lubeck

Scripture as Communication: Introducing Biblical Hermeneutics by Jeannine K. Brown

What Is the Bible and How Do We Understand It? by Dennis R. Edwards

Words of Delight: A Literary Introduction to the Bible by Leland Ryken

About the Author

KAT ARMSTRONG was born in Houston, Texas, where the humidity ruins her Mexi-German curls. She is a powerful voice in our generation as a sought-after Bible teacher. She holds a master's degree from Dallas Theological Seminary and is the author of *No More Holding Back*, *The In-Between Place*, and the **Storyline Bible Studies**. In 2008, Kat cofounded the Polished Network to embolden working women in their faith and work. Kat is pursuing a doctorate of ministry in New Testament context at Northern Seminary and is a board member of the Polished Network. She and her husband, Aaron, have been married for twenty years; live in Dallas, Texas, with their son, Caleb; and attend Dallas Bible Church, where Aaron serves as the lead pastor.

KATARMSTRONG.COM
@KATARMSTRONG1

THESTORYLINEPROJECT.COM
@THESTORYLINEPROJECT

Notes

LESSON ONE | YOUR WORTHINESS COMES FROM GOD'S FAITHFULNESS

1. Jesudason Baskar Jeyaraj, "Genesis," in *South Asia Bible Commentary: A One-Volume Commentary on the Whole Bible*, ed. Brian Wintle (Grand Rapids, MI: Zondervan, 2015), 46.

2. Leland Ryken, *Words of Delight: A Literary Introduction to the Bible*, 2nd ed. (Grand Rapids, MI: Baker Academic, 1992), 74.

3. Robert Alter, *The Art of Biblical Narrative*, rev. ed. (New York: Basic Books, 2011), 66.

4. Jeyaraj, "Genesis," in *South Asia Bible Commentary*, 47.

5. Walter Brueggemann, *Genesis: A Bible Commentary for Teaching and Preaching* (Atlanta: John Knox Press, 1982), 243.

6. Richard Bauckham, *Who Is God?: Key Moments of Biblical Revelation* (Grand Rapids, MI: Baker Academic, 2020), 9.

7. Bauckham, *Who Is God?*, 8.

8. Kat Armstrong, *The In-Between Place: Where Jesus Changes Your Story* (Nashville: W Publishing, 2021), 30–35.

9. My view of Jacob's pillar of stone as an altar is supported by several commentaries. Walter Brueggemann refers to the pillar as a "shrine" and treats the words *pillar* and *altar* as interchangeable when referencing this biblical account; *Genesis*, 247, 283. Richard Bauckham also calls Jacob's Bethel pillar an altar and a temple for God; *Who Is God?*, 14–15.

10. John H. Sailhamer, *The Pentateuch as Narrative: A Biblical-Theological Commentary* (Grand Rapids, MI: Zondervan Academic, 1992), 202.

11. Bauckham, *Who Is God?*, 23.

LESSON TWO | YOUR FORGIVENESS COMES FROM GOD'S STEADFAST LOVE

1. P. G. George and Paul Swarup, "Exodus," in *South Asia Bible Commentary: A One-Volume Commentary on the Whole Bible*, ed. Brian Wintle (Grand Rapids, MI: Zondervan, 2015), 126.
2. Dennis T. Olson, "Exodus," in *Theological Bible Commentary*, eds. Gail R. O'Day and David L. Petersen (Louisville, KY: Westminster John Knox Press, 2009), 38–39.

LESSON THREE | YOUR PROGRESS COMES FROM GOD'S POWER

1. Lissa M. Wray Beal, *Joshua*, The Story of God Bible Commentary (Grand Rapids, MI: Zondervan Academic, 2019), 48.
2. Amy C. Cottrill, "Joshua," in *Women's Bible Commentary*, 3rd ed., eds. Carol A. Newsom, Sharon H. Ringe, and Jacqueline E. Lapsley (Louisville, KY: Westminster John Knox Press, 2012), 103.
3. K. Jesurathnam, "Joshua," in *South Asia Bible Commentary: A One-Volume Commentary on the Whole Bible*, ed. Brian Wintle (Grand Rapids, MI: Zondervan, 2015), 271.
4. Beal, *Joshua*, 48–49.
5. Beal, *Joshua*, 113.

LESSON FOUR | YOUR RESCUE COMES FROM JESUS' RESURRECTION

1. Jordan K. Monson, "My Boss Is a Jewish Construction Worker," *Christianity Today*, November 22, 2021, https://www.christianitytoday.com/ct/2021/december/jewish-construction-worker-jesus -vocation-profession-stone.html.
2. Monson, "My Boss," *Christianity Today*.
3. Richard B. Hays, *Echoes of Scripture in the Gospels* (Waco, TX: Baylor University Press, 2016), 172.

LESSON FIVE | YOUR PURPOSE COMES FROM THE CHURCH'S POSITION

1. N. T. Wright and Michael F. Bird, *The New Testament in Its World: An Introduction to the History, Literature, and Theology of the First Christians* (Grand Rapids, MI: Zondervan Academic, 2019), 757.
2. D. A. Carson and Douglas J. Moo, *An Introduction to the New Testament*, 2nd ed. (Grand Rapids, MI: Zondervan, 2005), 636.
3. Larry George, "1 Peter," in *True to Our Native Land: An African American New Testament Commentary*, ed. Brian K. Blount (Minneapolis: Fortress Press, 2007), 481.
4. Othmar Keel, *The Symbolism of the Biblical World: Ancient Near Eastern Iconography and the Book of Psalms*, trans. Timothy J. Hallett (Winona Lake, IN: Eisenbrauns, 1997), 181.